BROKE TO A QUARTER MILLION

The Point is Not to Work, It's to Generate Income

Gualter Amarelo

Copyright © 2019 **Gualter Amarelo**

All rights reserved.

This document is geared towards providing exact and reliable information in regards to the topic and issue covered.

No part of this book may be reproduced in any form or by any electronic or mechanical means including information storage and retrieval systems, without permission in writing from the author. The only exception is by a reviewer, who may quote short excerpts in a review.

The trademarks that are used are without any consent, and the publication of the trademark is without permission or backing by the trademark owner. All trademarks and brands within this book are for clarifying purposes only and are owned by the owners themselves, not affiliated with this document.

Contents

ACKNOWLEDGEMENTS	4
INTRODUCTION	5
CHAPTER 1	**33**
MY FIRST HOME WAS A DUD	33
CHAPTER 2	**59**
LET'S DO IT AGAIN	59
CHAPTER 3	**71**
FINANCIAL FREEDOM	71
CHAPTER 4	**81**
DIVORCE & BETRAYAL	81
CHAPTER 5	**101**
THE YEAR OF THE COMEBACK	101
CHAPTER 6	**117**
A LESSON LEARNED	117
CHAPTER 7	**127**
ONE LAST HURDLE	127
OUTROS	139

ACKNOWLEDGEMENTS

Thanks to my awesome brother, Owner of AMP Academy LLC, author, and ghostwriter of this book, Joshua Amarelo.

Thanks to my mentors, who are too numerous to name and who continue to inspire me every day and teach me new ways to grow my business and help others.

Thanks to my friends who were inspired by my story and encouraged me to put this book together for this story to come out.

Thank you to all the people who believed in me even when I had trouble believing in myself, who pushed me to become the man that I am today, allowing me to help more people than I ever thought possible.

INTRODUCTION

Here's the thing. I went from being worth nothing—divorced, broken-hearted, dead broke and living off my little brother's charity in 2014—to being worth a quarter million dollars in only two years. Beyond that, I follow a strategy that allows me double my income year-to-year. Let me introduce myself: My name is Gualter Amarelo, real estate agent, property manager, real estate investor, and now, your real estate mentor.

Not long ago, I was driving around my hometown with my buddy Bruno. I forget exactly what he'd asked me, but it led us into one of my favorite topics: real estate. During our discussion, Bruno asked me some really important questions and I realized that if I wanted to add value to the lives of people all around the world, same thing I've dreamed of doing since I was little, I needed to make this information available to everybody, not only the people in my hometown.

Throughout this book, I'm going to address some of the significant questions Bruno brought up that day.

I guess my life story is about how you can come from nothing and still achieve success. I'd always wanted to be successful and have an impact on the lives of everybody I came into contact with—just about everyone wants this. So when I was younger, my brother and some friends and I started a band with me on the bass. Our original band didn't work out, so most of us moved on to trying covers, but we didn't have a passion for that and soon the bands had died. It was during my band days that I'd met my wife. The event of our encounter took place when I was working at Walmart. She was dating one of the managers at the time, and I remember telling my brother about this attractive new girl that worked in the layaway department.

It took about eight years of friendship and support as she went through a breakup and then another; but in the end, we'd both fallen madly in love with one another and on September 10, 2011, we got married, surrounded by family and friends in the backyard of my very first house, which we'd bought together a few years earlier, by my father, a man whom I love and adore more than any words could ever describe.

Back to my car ride with Bruno. It was a beautiful spring day, the sun was shining and there was a cool breeze that whispered life and opportunity as we drove by City Hall with its nearly two dozen flags from various countries blowing in the wind, commemorating the melting pot that was our city of Fall River, MA. I had picked him up because his BMW had gotten a flat tire and I'd offered to fill it for him – he was shocked that I knew how to do that. I'll never forget that moment as we passed by Dunny's Saloon, one of my favorite bars in Fall River, and Bruno turned to me, and that's where this all started.

"So, I have to ask: Your parents were rich, right?"

I want to be very clear about this because I get asked it a lot and it's important for people to know that you don't need to have rich parents to be successful. By no means was my family even remotely close to being rich. They had always been hard workers, yes. In fact, they're still working very hard. They've always had enough to get by, but by no means was my family *rich* at all. We were lower-middle class by the time my parents divorced and my brother and I moved into our own place together.

To give you a little insight into my childhood and home life, my father wasn't born in this country. He was born on the island of São Miguel in the Azores and my grandparents came to America in search of better income when my father was only six years old. They worked in the city's factories. They were mill workers. My grandfather drove forklifts at Quaker Fabric and my grandmother sewed for the same company. My father, who had two kids by the time he was twenty-five, was twenty-one when he married an eighteen-year-old woman—who would be my mother. They married young and had no college education. They didn't even have the means to pursue a college education if they'd wanted to. They went to high-school, sure, but my mother dropped out of that. That's right, I have an immigrant and a high-school dropout for parents. They were very smart in a lot of ways, particularly with parenting, but formal education wasn't something they had.

They weren't taught how to pursue wealth, and so they never passed along the knowledge to me.

"Oh, wow. So, were they involved in real estate, then?"

Nope. They weren't involved in real estate either. The only history my family has with real estate is that my Portuguese grandparents who spoke heavily broken English in the long run, after years and years of saving up money, bought a four-family home in the city of Fall River—I was raised there. My parents never owned a house when I was growing up. My father had wanted to buy a home, and I found out recently that my mother had considered getting into real estate, but she never took the test to get her license and that dream died along with my parents' marriage. For the entire time I was building an empire, the only piece of property my family owned was my grandparents' multifamily building.

So, there you go again—*no*—without doubt, they weren't rich, and they had very little exposure to real estate.

As I mentioned, I did grow up in my grandparents' four-family home, so that was I picture I forever had in my head. Like, my grandfather was my landlord – I knew that. I knew that landlords seemed to have money, but I didn't indeed grasp what that meant nor why until I was much older. I had a simple knowledge that my grandfather was a landlord and I wasn't allowed to do certain things in the house, like jump around or play tag with my brother, or make too much noise, because we had neighbors upstairs and my grandmother downstairs worked overnights. However, I do remember a lot of my friends didn't have those rules, but it was a part of my life. I was a kid. I didn't really worry about it. It was a mere situation that existed and I didn't try to question it. Follow the rules, and everything is great.

One thing I did question, though, was why my father always had to work. My mom used to call him a workaholic. She would stay home with us; meanwhile, my father always had two or three jobs. He was busting his butt and I remember there always being a lot of tension in the house about money because it was always scarce. It always seemed it was disappearing.

There wasn't enough. We had food budgets and there was never anything extra to get me and my brother toys or even Fruit Roll-ups once in a while. It was always no-name-brand cereal or oatmeal.

There was only ever enough money to get by, never anything extra to save or plan for the future. Growing up, my little brother and I always just assumed that's how life was. Even our friends' parents had their own homes and were always working extra jobs and barely scraping by with enough to live a life well below luxury. We didn't know anything different. We knew that we had to go to school and we had to get good grades and one day we'd get a good job. I remember thinking, "Okay, my dad makes $40,000 a year, so that's what I want to make. If I make that, I'll be all set. If I make that, I'll be doing really good, just like my dad."

My mother had put a lot of things in my head, like I wasn't allowed to start dating until I had $30,000 in the bank. She set me up with these weird rules: I couldn't date somebody until I was ready to marry them, and I couldn't marry them until I was ready to buy a house. I believed that a house was purchased with a 20% downpayment, which meant I had to have $30,000 in the bank. This was the math I'd had in my head ever since I was fifteen. Those were the sorts of thoughts in my head.

Here I was, fifteen years old, and my parents have never owned a house. They had gotten married without even plans of owning a house. When I asked about that, she told me I should buy one because that was the mistake they had made.

I remember making a decision then never to make the same mistakes as my parents.

Another key benefit is that my father used to always tell me that real estate was the key to getting rich. "The rich get richer and the poor stay poor, and the rich own real estate." He'd always said that. He always told me, "You need to work hard, work hard, work hard, save your money, and then invest it."

My father was a very smart man. So why did he never end up getting rich? Why don't I come from wealth when my father was so smart? The funny thing is that they both knew, they both gave me the seeds, they both told me to invest, but my father never invested and my mother never invested. To this day, despite my success, they've still never invested, though my father recently got his real estate license and I couldn't be more proud of him taking that first step to financial freedom. As of February 2018, my father joined my team of real estate agents and we're going to start working together doing some flips and doing some of the kinds of work that I do already.

But it's interesting, you know. To think that I didn't come from real estate. Nor did I come from any kind of money whatsoever. But I *did* come from a strong work ethic and a promise to not make the mistakes of my parents. That, I consider, was one of the beginning pieces that set me up to succeed in life.

"So, where did you go to school?"

Well, that's another funny story. I really didn't have the typical school experience. I grew up in Fall River and started out attending Belisle Elementary School (now torn down and developed into single family homes), but I stopped after the second grade. There was some sort of situation – I barely remember it – and my parents decided to pull my brother and I out of school. It was over some school assignment that my mother felt was an invasion of privacy. The assignment was, "I love my parents, but sometimes they do weird things, like _____.", and then you filled in the blank. Mine was innocent—my mother had promised to take me to cash a check, but then she forgot—written in true 7-year-old fashion with half the letters backwards and every eight or ninth letter sitting on the line. My childlike schoolwork wasn't like anything half the class had written though. Someone from the class had written about a domestic dispute and another had written about her mommy's friend that visited when daddy was out. You know, invasion of privacy kind of things.

That assignment was the catalyst that changed me from being like everybody else. My mom decided that she was pulling her kids out of school and she was going to homeschool us. *My mother* – the high-school dropout. Because, you know, dropping out in the tenth grade clearly means you're qualified to handle your children's intellectual futures.

Now, the benefit of homeschooling is obviously not in the social aspect of things since it was just my brother and I. We were fortunate enough to have some very close friends from back in school who we're still friends with to this day – in fact, two of them got married within the past five years and the best of them all just got married in 2017. Best wishes, friends! They lived next door and their parents were best friends with our parents. So, I didn't grow up having great social skills either – that was something I had to really work on as a young adult.

Initially, I was an introvert, and till date, I still have some introverted tendencies, but largely, I've become a social creature and I love spending time with others, sharing the knowledge I've gained and creating new experiences with all the fascinating people I meet on a daily basis.

Nowadays, you can find me speaking in front of fifty to a hundred people without breaking a sweat. I genuinely enjoy getting in front of people and having these conversations. But I had to build that. Being homeschooled put me at a disadvantage in the social sphere, but it also instilled some respectable qualities in me and my brother. We found that we could learn absolutely anything if we wanted the knowledge badly enough. We even learned that the social detriments of homeschooling could be learned away. You don't always have to be told or taught something by somebody else. You just have to make the decision to do something, then you have to go out and dig for the information on your own.

Our mom couldn't answer all our questions. Being a high-school dropout meant that mom didn't know certain levels of Math. Same for certain levels of History, or English, or Science. Throughout most of our homeschooling, my brother and I had to go back through the book and try to figure it out on our own. The answer was in there. It must have been. They wouldn't have given us the question if they hadn't told us how to get the answer. So, that digging for knowledge and finding the appropriate resources was something we learned to do at a very young age. We can't always rely on others to give us the information we need — sometimes we have to go out and get it ourselves. That was by far one of the greatest lessons I learned being homeschooled, and it's the one I still use to this day that has gotten me to my current level of success and will continue to get me to every advanced stage of success. When I don't know something, I just need to dig for the answer. All the answers are out there somewhere – they just need to be found, and I'm going to find them—all the answers, all the knowledge.

That was one of the strengths of my homeschooling. Now, obviously not everybody comes out of homeschooling with that value and that lesson. I'm not saying to go homeschool your children and they'll be successful. What I'm saying is that I turned a weakness into a positive skill. My mother couldn't teach me, so I had to learn on my own. I wasn't socially excellent at that time in my life, but I made myself a social person by putting myself into social situations that forced me out of my comfort zone.

Finding the information wasn't always easy either. We're talking about a time when the internet was in its early stages, but my family couldn't afford it, so we didn't have it. Instead, my brother and I were forced to find the answers we needed in good old fashioned hardcover encyclopedias and dictionaries. Eventually, we did have computers, but most of our schooling was based on encyclopedias and the text books my parents were able to afford. My education came from going through these books that she would buy each year and then taking some tests at the end of the year to evaluate and make sure that we knew what we were doing, because the state does like to know that homeschooled kids are getting at least some kind of education.

"Do you have a college degree?"

The answer used to embarrass me every time the question came up. "Did you go to college?" Yes. Sort of. I went to college for two semesters. During that time, I had a 4.0 GPA because I didn't go to college right away. I know that sounds counterintuitive, but hear me out.

I finished homeschooling and jumped right into work. You have to remember, I was always told to work hard, work hard, work hard, and save, then invest. So, I'd actually been working since I was twelve years old. My first job was at a Christian bookstore, putting prices on things and cleaning and other minor tasks. My second job was similar at first – I worked at a flooring company as a salesfloor assistant until I was moved over to work in the warehouse. My brother worked here with me, but he was moved into the estimating office. People sometimes ask if that bothered me; it didn't. Office work never seemed like real work to me. Remember, work hard, work hard, work hard, and save, then invest. My grandparents worked in factories. My father worked as an industrial painter and welder before managing a warehouse space at Walmart. So for me, working in the warehouse was following in my father's footsteps. Work hard, work hard, work hard, and save, then invest.

At eighteen, I started working at Walmart too and thought I was "the man". Within six months, I'd become a department manager. Six months after that, I'd become a department manager in a different department, and I was doing remarkable, working hard, working hard, working hard, for $10 an hour. Which was fine, because I did save, and I was able to buy a truck that I still have to this day, and I was happy. Once I bought that truck, though, my bank account stopped going up, and I hated that. When I finally saw my bank account after a year, again at $38, I decided that I needed to do something. Ten dollars an hour wasn't enough, especially if I wanted to start dating. By that time, my parents had already gotten divorced and that meant that the $30,000 savings before dating rule no longer held any power, so I had a girlfriend, but I still wanted to be able to have that money, because that's what I was told success was. So I made a commitment and I made a change.

At twenty-one, I got a new job making eighteen bucks an hour. Who cared that it was an incredibly hard labor job, working third shift in what felt like a sweat shop? I worked in shipping and receiving at a bakery, where the temperature could get up to a hundred and twenty degrees, and it did, almost every night in the summer. By the time I got home, I was heat-exhausted and sleep deprived every day. It put a damper on my social life. I hung out with friends less because I had to sleep to prepare for the hard night's work ahead of me. It put a strain on my romantic relationship because my girlfriend hated that I always wanted to sleep when she wanted for us to go out and do things.

But I learned hard work. I learned dedication. I learned how to put up with all the crazy overtime. And I learned that I hated it. I love hard work, but I hated physical labor because it didn't allow for much creativity, and because I couldn't be my authentic self nor follow my genuine passion.

My "new" girlfriend at the time saw that I hated it and finally suggested, "Hey, you know what, if you don't like that, why don't you go to college? Why don't you get a degree?" I thought it through and realized she was right. I didn't want hard labor. I wanted to supervise, like I was doing at Walmart. So, I started at my local community college, going for business management and marketing. After two semesters, I ended up getting an accounting job up near Boston, an hour away. And I drove there, 2-3 hours a day, 5 days a week for four years. My new girlfriend's (and future wife's) father had helped me secure a great accounting job, so I never completed that degree program, but I got enough education to get me into a job. Between college and my accounting job, I learned management, accounting, and marketing, all of which I still use today.

Like I said, I used to be embarrassed when I told people I didn't have a degree, but now I realize that it was never about getting a college degree for me. It was always about getting what I needed to build a business, because I always knew I was going to be a business owner. I didn't know what kind of business it would be, but I knew that owning a business was my goal. So, no to the college degree.

Now I say, you know what, if you don't have a degree, good. You're in the same spot as me. You can succeed because you don't have a degree and you haven't gotten all that bad programming of just study, study, study, and do nothing with it. And if you do have a degree, you can still break that programming and reprogram yourself to be successful beyond what a college degree could ever prepare you for.

"So, what did you do before this?"

I kind of preluded this when I was talking about my lack of college, but that wasn't where things picked up for me. I started in retail, then went into retail management, then into physical labor, then finance as a billing representative for a computer company near Boston. After getting married to the girl of my dreams, I worked for Johnson & Johnson for a short time. I realized that whenever I would jump from one company to another, I'd gotten a pay raise. I'd be doing less work, but because I had a different title, I could update my resume and I'd be able to get paid more, so I started doing that. I said, okay, this company's willing to pay me this at this title, so here I'm a billing representative, but now at Johnson & Johnson I'm an excel specialist. Boom, that jumped me up. Then I slid over to Coca-Cola as a planning analyst, looking at spreadsheets to see what needed to be done and then putting information into a computer so the machines would do it, and that got me another raise. Soon after that, Johnson & Johnson called me back and wanted to give me an administrative assistant position for the vice president of sales, so I went back to Johnson & Johnson, and I got another raise to just book their flights, pay their credit cards, and other little stuff like that.

That was my career, taking all different but similar jobs and getting bumps in pay each time. Finally, I realized again that I really, really, really, *really* hated doing that. I hated doing the tedious things. Some people love doing that stuff. Not me. I hated it so much that I hate doing it for myself, and yet I was doing it for a living. That's what triggered me to get out. I was making $70,000 a year and my expenses were well under that. I probably spent $30,000 a year, *maybe*. I lived off about two thousand dollars a month between my first mortgage and utilities. My trusty truck was long paid off at this time and was still running like a dream for the most part. So I had this exorbitant amount of money that was going into savings every year. I just didn't need it. I was always a $40,000 per year person. Then I suddenly started making all this money and I started buying real estate because that made sense to me at the time. I said, "I'm going to replace my funds with real estate."

"When was the moment you knew there was more?"

I remember it was a super-hot day, like extremely hot. Sweat was pouring down my face and I had taken off my shirt, which was only about 30% fabric while the other 70% was soaked from my body and begging me to go back inside to my air conditioning, as I mowed the lawn in the backyard of my first ever single-family home. I'd bought the home when I was twenty-two years old with my girlfriend. It was in that home that we'd spent months sleeping in the kitchen as we renovated the place to be the perfect dwelling for our little family, just me and her with our two dogs and cat. It was in that home that I'd proposed to her, and it was in that very backyard that I'd married her, vowing our lives to one another's happiness and devoting everything I did to making her every dream come true.

I was cutting the grass and I remember having the distinct thought, *"Yeah, I'm the lord of the land."* It was a reference to something my grandfather used to say. You remember, the grandfather who came over from the Azores and bought a multifamily house? That one. "I'm the lord of the land", he used to say it and remind me the tenants paid him rent. In that moment it hit me, I have all this land – it's all mine and nobody's paying me rent. I'm working and I'm paying a mortgage of $1,400 a month. I've got to pay the water bill. I've got to pay the electric bill. I've got to pay for overhead. I've got to maintain the lawn, and the lawn mower, plants, trees and the fences. I'm doing all this work, but all I have is a house. Where's the money? Why did I buy this thing that doesn't pay me?

My grandfather was the "lord of the land" and people were paying him to live there, paying him to do all that work. What kind of a lord was I, doing all the work and paying for the pleasure of doing it all myself? He's a landlord and I'm a landlord, but he's getting paid and I'm not.

I remember having this very frustrating conversation in my head, where I was just very upset with myself for putting myself into a situation where I spent all this money on something that wasn't benefitting my life. It made me feel like I had accomplished something because that's what society teaches us – that if you buy your own home you're successful – but it didn't actually pay me. I was stuck working because of this house. That moment was a punch in the gut so hard that I lost my breath and realized that I didn't want to do this anymore. What were my options, then?

"What about stocks?"

I did some minor stock trading here and there for a while when I was still at Johnson & Johnson, but I kept getting my account frozen due to day trading regulations and not being an accredited invest at the time.

Cryptocurrency is big now with Bitcoin on the rise and everybody is coming up to me saying, "What about Bitcoin? Are you in this? What do you think?" As far as the stock market I invest in Real Estate Investment Trusts (REIT's) because I understand real estate.

I'll tell you the same thing that Warren Buffet says to everybody, which is this: I don't understand it and I'm not going to get into it until I do. I'm not going to invest in it because I don't know how it works. There's money that's being made in cryptocurrency, yes, absolutely. If you understand it and you trust it, definitely, go for it. But if you don't understand it, you can't trust it, and you shouldn't invest in it.

Real estate, I understand. I understand it very well, so real estate is where I invest. I can make money no matter what the market's doing, and so that's what I do.

Like I said, I tried day trading for a while, but the problem was that I would make a little bit of money, then do something dumb and lose it, then I'd make a little bit of money, then do something dumb and lose it, and I did that all the time. I couldn't control whether it was going up or down. I couldn't add value to the company, so it wasn't something I could fix when it went wrong. With real estate, though, I can really get into a property and turn it into something else. I can make money a different way. I can adjust the use. I can fix it, renovate it, and increase rents. There's all sorts of different things you can do to a property to make sure that it generates extra income.

In real estate, you have control of whether you win or lose.

"So why real estate?"

Another big part of it was that I read in a blog that 80% of millionaires made their money through real estate, and that seemed like good math to me. I figured if 80% of them were doing it with real estate, I wasn't going to try what the other 20% were doing. It's possible, apparently, but it seems like the success rate is lower in cryptocurrency and owning companies. But real estate covered 80% of millionaires, and I decided to go with the better odds. Pareto's Principle is the 80/20 rule, and I decided the eighty made more sense.

I went after real estate and found it fascinating. When I made the decision to get into real estate, I started talking about it to everyone and saw the Law of Attraction at work. Real estate connections started popping up everywhere. I was working at Johnson & Johnson and I mentioned to a woman I worked with that I was getting interested in real estate, and she said, "Oh, my husband is a real estate investor. In fact, he used to manage a hundred properties. We own a place in Florida, Boston, on the Cape, and we can live in any one of them at any time. They're worth well over a million dollars and everything's pretty much taken care of by our tenants."

I was enthralled. I could tell my mouth was agape and my eyes were filled with the fire and fascination I still hold today. In that moment, I realized what I had always known but always doubted: "Oh, my God, this is real?" People actually make money in real estate and they're millionaires. They have homes in all these amazing places and they can just decide, I'm going to go live in Florida for a while, or on the Cape, or in Boston. It was a ground-shattering moment for me.

I was reading all these articles and blogs online, listening to podcasts and watching all kinds of YouTube videos, studying and building a spreadsheet with all these numbers, but they all felt fake until I finally met her husband.

He discussed with me so many things, like GRM, cap rates and a thousand other things in those conversations we had. I didn't understand a thing he was saying, but my homeschooling kicked in and I realized that if he could do it, then I could, and all I needed to do was dig deep enough for the right information.

So I started digging, and he was my first mentor. People ask me all the time what kind of guru's and classes I took to get into real estate. I didn't. While guru's and classes do have their place, I truly believe that mentorship and coaching are far more valuable. For me, I knew that I wanted to learn and I didn't have money to take all kinds of classes, so I started digging online, reading books, and I started to get involved with people who owned real estate.

When I met somebody who owned property, I took them out for lunch and asked them all kinds of questions: What do you know? How can I get more knowledge about this? When I took my coworker's husband out to lunch, I asked him all those questions. Thanks to him I met great friends and my first investor agent and my second real estate mentor – Jim Baptista.

Jim was phenomenal. He owned a bunch of property and he was willing to take me under his wing, to show me the ropes and help me get started with investing. Jim was the incredible real estate agent that helped me buy my first investment property after my wife and I sold our single-family home. I worked with Jim on buying my second property also, and he mentored me as an agent when I got my real estate license not long after. I look back and know that I wouldn't be the success I am today if it wasn't for Jim being in my life. I'm lucky enough to still have him in my life. Sometimes he'll call me up to check in on me and see how things are going and even though I may own more property than he does right now, I still like to call him to check in and see what I'm doing wrong or what I'm doing right because he's always been a genuinely good person and I know I owe a huge part of my success to him.

So, the mentors in my life, they're huge and I genuinely appreciate the people who stepped up for me. At this point in my career, I've had many different mentors, and I'll have had hundreds more by the time I die, but there's quite a few now who've really helped me get to where I am. Finding the right mentor will take you a long way in your road to success, and by picking up this book, I can tell you're ready to begin. So let's do this!

-A Mentor is someone who is far ahead of you and has the life or business that you desire. Seek out mentors now and often.

CHAPTER 1

MY FIRST HOME WAS A DUD

I made the unforgivable mistake of going into my first home purchase uninformed. I bought the house in 2008 – for those of you who don't know, 2008 was far from the best time to buy. The real estate market started crashing right around 2007, and in 2008 it started to tank. I saw all these foreclosures and short sales and thought, *"This is it! This is the time to buy! Look, everything is going down. I need to jump in before it goes back up!"*

I was working up near Boston at this point and I lived in Fall River with a one-hour commute each way, so I decided to move to a city that was between Fall River and Boston so I'd be closer to work but still close to my family and the city that I love. I bought a single-family home in a city I had never lived in before – Taunton, MA. Taunton is a great place, but I didn't know it and my real estate agent didn't know it. This was before I met Jim. My real estate agent at the time was getting frustrated with me and my future wife because she was showing us all these different foreclosures and different things. She was a sweetheart, but I get it – she was trying to find us a place for $120,000 that wasn't a $120,000 house, and it wasn't working. Finally, I told her to start searching for up to $180,000 houses, and the search was going a little better, but there were still houses that were missing pipes or were too small or whose yards were too small. Every single house had massive compromises.

As a real estate agent now, I have a name for what people like me and my girlfriend were looking for at the time – we were people looking for a "unicorn". We wanted the dream, the beautiful, magical and mythical creature and pure in all its magnificence, that doesn't actually exist. We wanted the amazing deal, the beautiful house with a huge bathroom with two sinks and a massive yard closed off from any neighbors, and we wanted it with a very small budget. We figured we'd just fix things. HGTV syndrome.

I had watched hundreds of episodes of different shows on HGTV with my girlfriend by my side. In fact, that was one of our favorite things to do – cuddle up on the couch with some tortilla chips, dip and watch HGTV. We used to joke about how we were in one of those episodes. We went to a house and said, "Well, we could do this! We could do that! We can blow all this out. It's going to be amazing!" But we learned. Slowly, over time, we learned. I was a slow learner back then – I had in my head that we were going to find an amazing deal on a single-family, and I wouldn't stray from that.

Of course, then I wizened up and we did stray from that. We eventually upped our price to the whopping $220,000 range, and magically the houses got significantly better. The houses were bigger. The yards were bigger. For me back then it was important to have a big yard, though now I look back and don't understand it. A bigger yard means lots of maintenance. Back then, it was important to me because I was a hard worker and I liked the idea of making my yard a haven the same way my grandfather had, pruning fruit trees, planting a huge garden, trimming faces into the bushes, the patio, the grapevine, the perfect landscaping with everything immaculately manicured. I wanted a big garage so I could work on cars, even though I've never liked working on cars – it was something my father did, so I wanted to have the option. Those were the things that were important to me. The house? I didn't care much about that. I was a hard worker. I could fix anything.

So, we found this house that was the best one in a decent neighborhood. It was a real fixer-upper, but we ended up getting a great deal on it. It was on the market for $220,000 and our real estate agent advised putting an offer in at $200,000, but I knew it was a short sale. I thought an offer closer to $180,000 would be good, but our agent said, "No way, that's going to make them really angry. They aren't going to like that." After counseling with my girlfriend, we decided to put in an offer at $170,000. We could tell our agent wasn't looking out for us and we decided to put in a crazy low offer.

Just so you all know, a good agent will never tell you what she told us. A good agent would never say, "That's not a good idea when the market is just turning." A good agent will say, "Let's put in the offer and if you get it, you get it. If you don't, you don't. Who cares?" I certainly didn't care if we got the house or not. It's not like it was our unicorn. We were settling.

So, we put the offer in at $170,000 and it went to the bank. The previous owner had been foreclosed, everything just falling apart and leaving the bank to watch the market turn down. From what the agent told me the bank folded and had to liquidate as they went out of business. To our amazement, the bank accepted our offer, which always made me wonder whether I should have asked for a bit less. It's all in the past and I got a great deal, but could I have gotten a better deal? Maybe $160,000? Maybe $150,000? I don't know.

Anyway, we got the house and I brought my uncle, who went to a vocational school for carpentry and has been a carpenter since he graduated from high school, to the house. He looked around and said, "Gualter, there is *a lot* of work here. This is a big project. It's a lot."

I said, "Yeah, we can do it, right? It's not that big of a deal. You're a carpenter and I'm willing to work." I've always been a hard worker.

My uncle looked around again said, sighing. "Look, if you want to do this, yeah, I'll help you."

My aunt was there too, and she looked at my uncle, her face had a mask of worry. She knew she wasn't going to see her husband for a long time. And she was right.

It was a 1,200 square foot home built in 1760, before America was free from England. It literally had the severed trunks of trees holding up the first floor in the basement and three different additions with crawl spaces. This place had been through a lot; it was a mess – it really was.

We spent the next four years renovating the heck out of it. While the market was turning down, we were dumping money into this house and trying to bring the value up. In fact, if I'm being honest, I think most of the time I didn't even care about the value of the house – I was just trying to make it what I wanted it to be, what my girlfriend wanted it to be. I wanted to give her the home she had always dreamed about. My entire family supported me in this. My grandfather came and showed me how to do things in the yard. My dad, brother and friends came to help me tear down walls and put up new drywall and plaster and sand and paint and put up moldings. We filled trash bags with old insulation and chunks of horsehair plaster and filled dumpsters with all the refuse of a madman working on a mad project.

My girlfriend wanted everything new, so we ripped out all the paneling, ripped out the wooden beams, repaired the floors that were crooked and sagging. My uncle helped me raise the second floor so we could replace all the ceiling joists and pull out the column that was sitting awkwardly in the middle of the kitchen. We leveled the whole thing out, putting in new LVL beams all the way across, straightening out the hardwood floors on the second floor. We raised the ceiling on the second floor from six feet to eight feet so my head wasn't dragging across the ceiling every time I walked. I even added these awesome lights at the top and bottom of the closet so we could see at night – they doubled as some pretty good mood lighting when the times were right. We put in baffles and vents and insulated the entire thing, framed it all out, did everything a hundred percent up to code. My grandmother and mother put aside their differences and came together to help clean the house to pristine conditions when we'd finished tearing the place apart and putting it back together.

My uncle was there with me for weeks and weeks and weeks. Every weekend, he came over, worked for twelve hours each day, and on Sundays, he would give me a big list of things to do during the week to prepare for our next big task the following weekend. When I got home from work after my hour-long drive, I would work four to six hours on that list. Sometimes I'd get up early and work on some stuff after I'd gotten ready for my office job. More than once I had to use a lint roller to get the dust off my clothes before work. My dad was there every weekend and some nights during the week, teaching me to run electrical wires and plumbing, all the things he'd learned from his own father when they'd renovated my grandparents' house. My dad and uncle taught me how to insulate, how to frame, how to hang drywall, how to mud. Between the two of them, they knew everything in the trade.

I'll never forget one of the moments I respected my uncle the most. We were lifting the second floor to replace the joists and we ended up having to cut the drywall to allow the house to lift the amount we needed because the jacks kept kicking out downstairs. As we were cutting through the drywall, my uncle accidentally cut through one of the water lines for the radiators, causing water to spray everywhere, soaking the second floor and the kitchen underneath.

He was devastated. "I've been in the trade for 27 years and I've never cut a pipe, but in my own nephew's house, I cut a pipe?" He was sad and embarrassed.

Honestly, he cared more than I did. I was just happy having my family there helping me with these crazy projects, putting in unbelievable amounts of effort to make sure my girlfriend and I had the amazing home I pictured this house could be. My uncle paid for the plumber against my wishes. He solved the whole problem and worked it all out. It was a project of passion and love between me and my entire family. I remember my grandmother, at almost seventy years old, grabbing huge heaps of wood and throwing them in a fire that was twice as tall as she was, then walking away to grab another. We all put so much into it and I can never find the words to thank them for everything they did for me. I have a lot of good memories in that house.

We'd put so much money into building up the value, far beyond the $8,500 downpayment and another $8,500 closing costs, which we paid because at that point I hadn't known having the seller pay that was an option. It was a short sale, obviously, so maybe they wouldn't have agreed to it anyway, but who would have known? My point is that we didn't know any better and our real estate agent wasn't taking care of us the way they should have. They weren't investors. They were just going through the motions, getting their commission check and never seeing us again. That's not the way it should be. A good real estate agent educates their buyers and sellers to make sure that they get the best end of every deal – that's how I train my students. That's why people know, that when they were with one of my students, they work with the best.

By the time we finished our renovations, we had no money left. We'd used it all, and when our roof started leaking, we had nothing left to fund a repair.

My grandmother, you remember the one who faced down a flaming mass twice her size as if she were some epic hero watching her enemy's fortress burn to the ground, came to me and said in her broken English, "Look, my grandson, we are going to take care of you. We have the money. We will pay for it. You have a contractor come and do it. We have enough going on with the rest of the project. We can't do the roof and all this. I'm going to pay a roofer to come do the roof for you. We'll keep doing the downstairs and the rest of the house."

That was the first time I ever borrowed money from my family. Ten thousand dollars I borrowed to finish the roof, and that was really tough for me, because I was a hard worker – I did everything for myself. I didn't like other people helping me financially. I've always worked hard for everything I have and I've always done it myself. The day I paid them back was the greatest feeling, knowing that I'd taken a loan from my grandparents and I'd paid it back when they hadn't expected me to pay it back. I earned it and I proved to them that I could handle it.

I know I'm giving a lot of detail about this house, but it's important for you to know that I made a lot of mistakes in this purchase, and I thought I was making all the right decisions at the time. At this point, I didn't have my mentors pointing me in the right direction, or even telling me how poor of an investment I had made. Yet at the same time, I wouldn't trade the experience for anything, because everything that could have been done in that house was done for me. My family took very, very good care, helping work, helping pay for things I couldn't afford. At the end of the day, if it didn't work out, it was on me, obviously, but it was nice knowing that my family was there to support me.

The unfortunate thing, though, was that I was dumping money into this bad investment. After doing the math, I found that the renovations cost roughly $20,000, plus the $17,000 we spent on the downpayment and closing costs. So we'd put $37,000 into the property that sold four years later at $34,000 more than when we bought it. We put a lot of love, sweat, tears, blood, and money into the house, and we lost $3,000 when we sold it, but we were just thankful to walk away with a check because 2012 was the absolute bottom of the market. We were lucky, because a lot of people lost even more than that.

I did the math – we spent 48 months paying a $1,500 mortgage and didn't quite break even when we sold the property, so that's a pretty bad investment. We could have rented an apartment for $1,000 a month without having to do all that work during the renovation period and saved $24,000. It was a very important lesson I learned: never own what you live in. Rent what you live in, and rent out what you own. It's a tough concept to grasp. Few people talk about it, but when you do the math, it cost me nearly $70,000 to live in that house between paying for renovations and paying a mortgage, which is no different than renting to own, despite that owning a home was supposedly the best investment a person could make.

This is the point where I was cutting the grass and realized the magnitude of my mistake. I wasn't the lord of the land – I was the lord of paying bills for a house. I went broke for the house. I started looking at all the deals around me. Again, this was in 2011, as the market was right around its lowest. I'd proposed to my girlfriend in 2010 and to my unspeakable happiness, she'd said yes. I started talking to my new fiancé, and I showed her the math I'd done and was telling her, "Come on, we've gotta do something. The house next door is only $80,000 right now."

At $80,000, I should have been able to buy it, renovate it just the way we renovated our own place, and sell it for a profit, or at least rent it out and make a killing that way. I started calling banks, "Hi, this is Gualter Amarelo. I own a property and work a full-time job, and my fiancé works a full-time job. We're ready to be real estate investors and want to buy our second home to flip it."

The bank said, "Yeah, okay. No problem. Do you have 20% down?"

I said, "No, but I was able to buy my first house with 3% down. Can we just do that again? That's the one I want to do."

The bank said, "You said you already own a home, so you can't do that again. You can't buy a second house with the FHA loan."

That drove me mad. Here I had an opportunity right in front of me, and I had $10,000 in my pocket, but it wasn't enough to get me an $80,000 house and pay for the renovations. At that time, I didn't know anything about hard money at the time. Even if I had known about it, I would have been too scared to do anything. I had no connections, so I had no way to do this. The houses, the deals, were all around me, and I couldn't do anything with them.

I decided, "Okay, fine, I won't do a flip. I'll buy a rental. I'll buy a three-family rental." So, I called up the same bank and said the same thing. "Hi, this is Gualter Amarelo. I own a property and work a full-time job, and my fiancé works a full-time job. We're ready to be real estate investors and want to buy a three-family rental property. I've got the 3% down-payment."

The bank said, "No, you can't do that either. The only way you can go and buy a three-family is if you sell your single family house."

At this point, I was thinking, "Perfect. Sell my single family house, buy a three-family, and then I can buy another single family house. Perfect plan. No problem. I've already renovated this thing and I'm bored with it anyway."

I went to my now wife and told her, "This is the plan. This is what we're going to do. Sell the house and move forward."

She said, "No, I love this house. We worked so hard to get it to this point. We're not selling it. You're crazy. I'll divorce you if you decide to do that."

And so I didn't decide to do that. I loved her more than the thought of selling the house. But now, I needed a new plan.

Another year I said this, trying to figure out a plan. "I have that garage that I wanted so badly, and I have a huge yard. I love the garage, and I love the cars being protected from new England weather, but if I move the driveway over in front of the house, I can split the land and build a house where my garage is." I started doing the research on plot plans and how I'd divide the property and what would be entailed and I realized it's a lot of work and, again, a lot of money which I didn't have. I still had that original $10,000 plus maybe another $4,000 that I'd saved up, but that wasn't going to cut it. The bank wouldn't give me a loan.

Again, I approached my wife. "Look, honey, I think it would be a great idea for us to sell this house. We could buy a three-family, live in it for a little while, and then we can go buy our single family, even bigger and better than this one. We'll be able to make enough money on the three-family that it can pay for our next house."

It took three months of such conversations for me to convince her, and she finally gave me the green light to look into selling the house.

I put it on Zillow, which I thought was the right move for us. I thought it was like a game – somebody made an offer and I accepted or declined, like filling out a checklist. Offer me $250,000, and I'll sell the house in a heartbeat.

I got a call from a real estate agent saying, "Hey, you know what, I think I've got somebody who would buy that house for $250,000."

I called my wife right away and told her, "Babe, they'll buy the house for $250,000."

There was no hesitation in her voice when she said, "Sell it."

The real estate agent came in, taking all kinds of pictures and saying, "This house is amazing! What a great house! You've done such an amazing job!" She made us feel really, really awesome about everything we'd done. We were thrilled. At the end, the real estate agent said, "You know what, I think I could sell this house for $230,000."

I looked at my wife and we were both pretty put off, but my wife was far more vocal than I was. "Wait, what? We didn't say $230,000. We said $250,000. There's not a buyer? You said there was a buyer who wanted to buy it right now. You're talking about putting it on the market? No way, we need 24 hours to think about this. We're not doing this."

I admired my wife's strength then, but as soon as the real estate agent left, she leaned hard into me. She was furious with me, and I was defensive because I didn't see it coming either. We were both mad at the real estate agent for having lied to us, but she was mad at me for putting us in this situation. It took a while, but at the end of the conversation, we did the math and figured that if we could get $230,000, it would still be worth it. We knew commissions were going to take us down to $220,000 and it was still all right for us, so we decided to put it on the market.

I was cutting the grass twice a week, and we were cleaning the house every single weekend to prepare for these open houses. It was a lot of work. Anybody who says selling your house is easy has never sold a house. By 2017, I had sold four of my own personal properties and it's stressful every single time, so I make sure that my students are honest with their sellers. "It's going to suck, but there's a reward at the end."

For three months our house was on the market and we were doing open houses all the time. Another friend of mine had bought a house at the same time that we had, and they decided to sell it the same time also. His house was already under agreement, and he'd made a $100,000 profit. Whereas we were barely going to break even.

We ended up selling the house for $208,000 and we had to put $5,000 toward the closing costs. In the end, we made $203,000. My note was somewhere around $166,000 remaining and we walked away with about $34,000 on the transaction. At least it was something. We'd spent $37,000 on renovations, but that was years ago. So at least $34,000 in our account right now can get us on to the next project.

By the time we sold the house, we hadn't found another place to live yet, so we ended up moving in with my father. His apartment was in my grandfather's four-family, with my grandparents downstairs, my dad living on the second floor with us, and my little brother living on the third floor – three generations of Amarelos living in the same building.

My dad's apartment was a pretty good size – 1,100 square feet with two parlors, three bedrooms, and my dad was going back and forth between spending nights at home and at his girlfriend's place. Despite all that space, it was still a very tight living situation, because all of our stuff was packed in front of his. We had rented a storage space for the bigger stuff, but our day-to-day things took up quite a bit of space, especially since we also owned a wedding invitation business at the time. Our computers and printers and cardstock and new invitation designs and all the other necessities took over the entire kitchen and the hallway connecting the two parlors.

My dad was way more patient than we had any right to ask of him as we ran a business and lived all in the space that he'd had completely to himself since my mom had left and my brother and I had moved out ten years earlier. My wife was stressed out and I could tell that she wasn't very happy with the living situation. This isn't the life I had promised her. I promised her a bigger house and instead we were living in a small apartment with my dad. Still, she tried not to complain. She excelled in the business and she took a great interest in making sure we were always at the showings when we were selling our house, and she was always looking for the perfect multi-family to get us going.

Finally, we did find a three-family and put in an offer on the same day we were moving into my dad's house. The trucks were half-full and I had a handful of family and friends helping to load it when I got the call from my new real estate agent, friend, and real estate investment mentor – you remember Jim? He called and said, "Hey, this is the one. You've got to get here now. There are 15 people here. If you don't get in here now, I'm going to buy it myself."

When your investment mentor tells you this is it, you have to go for it. Jim was the trigger. He was how I knew. It felt like we'd been to a hundred houses, and this was the one. I was hesitant to leave all my friends when they were helping me, but everyone told me not to be crazy. They knew how much I wanted this place, so they told me to go. And we did go.

We went and put in an offer on the house. It was accepted. We bought a three-family house for $157,000. What a deal! It took us ten months to close on that house, which we put under agreement the day we were moving into my dad's house. That meant that we were living with my dad for almost a year.

We thought at most it would be two months. We'd fixed everything and move into one of the units, and we'd keep on this journey we'd set out on to truly be a lord of the land (my dream) and eventually own our own beautiful single-family home once again – my wife's dream. Two months went by and we hadn't closed. It was torture, not knowing when it was going to close. Three, four, five, and we hadn't closed. My wife and I argued constantly, with her telling me that this was the dumbest thing we ever did. She'd trusted me and look where we were, living with my dad. We'd had a beautiful house. Our life was perfect. Now we were stressed and everything was falling apart.

But our life **wasn't** perfect. I wasn't happy with our situation. I wasn't happy having to work day after day, 40, 50, 60 hours a week, driving an hour each day to and from work, spending hours outside cutting the grass. It wasn't perfect.

Looking back, I think that's when things started to rot in our relationship. Those were really tough times between her and me, and with life in general. We were working these jobs that we hated, both driving an hour to work again. Strange as it is to say, though, I'm thankful for those moments, because it showed us who we were and what we actually had.

Eventually, ten months after going under agreement, we did close on the three-family house in September of 2013 after selling our single-family in 2012. Ten months of torture, waiting for the day it would close, and we finally closed.

As I was renovating the new place, I put in an offer and got another house under agreement – the two-family house right next door with a beautiful second floor. It was a 1,400 square foot apartment with two massive bedrooms, and it had the space for my wife's wedding invitation business. Everything was perfect in that unit, and I remember my wife and I having these massive arguments about being in my dad's house, cramped and stuck and unable to live our lives the way we'd gotten used to at our first house with its massive garage and all the space to ourselves.

The plan was to move into the two-family, which was supposed to close the day after the three-family, but they ran into some trouble separating the septic and had some other running water issues and they had to replace the roof. There were so many things that ended up pushing out the closing date. After how long it took to close on the three-family and how stressed out my wife was with the living situation, I said, "Look, babe, why don't we just move into the three-family? The closing already got pushed back again and we don't know when this two-family is going to close. We need our own space again."

My dad was absolutely amazing with letting us live at his place. He'd been patient and given us pretty much free reign. He'd started spending more time at some point at his girlfriend's so my wife and I could have our privacy. There was nothing that he'd done to inconvenience us. The problem was that half of our stuff was still packed in boxes because we didn't want to unpack only to pack up again. All our stuff was hidden behind boxes and the apartment was overly cluttered with all our stuff packed in front of things. It wasn't a comfortable way to live and I knew the strain this was putting on our marriage.

-Be aware of the strain your goals will put on the people closest to you.

Chapter 2

LET'S DO IT AGAIN

This chapter is all about my second investment property. After selling my single-family and having bought my first multi-family, I'd proven to myself that it worked. Literally two days after putting my first investment property under agreement, I started going after my second investment property – the two family next door. I realized I could buy two at once, so why shouldn't I? I had the money sitting there, so why not use it?

The three-family had cost me $12,000 out-of-pocket as my down-payment, so I had another $22,000 left sitting in the bank from selling my single-family, and roughly another $10,000 from saving up over the last four years. We'd saved a ton of money when we were living with my dad too, because he charged us very little rent when we were there, which allowed us to save money like crazy.

Now, this two-family wasn't advised by my family, nor my real estate agent, my mentor, nor my uncle. When I went into this building, it was rough. It needed a roof and the carpets were all covered with mold which was also in the ceilings and in the attic. The first floor had a tenant living there at the time – a mother and her son. The mother was a sweetheart, but her son was a scary-looking kid. There were holes in the walls from where he had punched them, the doors were broken, a fan blade had been ripped off the ceiling fan, the carpets were ripped up, the couches were broken and the fabric on them was torn. It was disgusting and the smell of smoke was everywhere. It looked like animals were living down there, like a frat house full of disrespectful college kids. It turned out the kid's father owned the building and his 18-year-old son and his friends were the ones living there, which was why the building was in such disrepair.

Since I was so distracted by the existing tenants and what they'd done to the home, I hadn't even noticed some of the major issues that were brought up during the home inspection. Despite all that, I didn't believe it was that bad. I figured a lot of it was cosmetics, and cosmetics are the easy part. Yeah, we'd need to put a new roof on it, but it wouldn't be terrible.

When the home inspector came, though, that's when we found all the mold in the attic, but the biggest expense was that the basement was actually dug out, but never reinforced. This is a little hard to explain, so let me draw you a picture. Imagine this: there was a crawl space about three feet high, and at some point, somebody thought, *"God, you know what I'd love? A full basement."* And then that person spent days and days drinking far too much alcohol as they tried to come up with a solution to their crawl space dilemma. Ultimately, that person decided, "Hey, why don't I just dig another four feet or so down and then I'll have my basement."

Then, without fully considering the ramifications of such an act, this person proceeded to dig out immense amounts of dirt to have a full basement. At some point, they then got frustrated and decided that a full-sized basement wasn't completely necessary and he could just stop digging. The foundation had been made of rocks stacked and held together by concrete, and many of those rocks had fallen out during the digging process, and the digger carefully placed them off to the side atop a mound of dirt. This was the condition of the basement of the two-family investment property that I was now considering purchasing.

The correct way to do what the digger wanted to do would have been to building a foundation out of cinder blocks, but obviously, that wasn't the path they chose, so there was a huge concern here. I got a quote of $25,000 to have a company come in, support the house, finish digging up the foundation, cement it on both sides, and then lower the house back into place. Way more than I expected to spend.

I ended up going back to the seller, who had the house on the market for $130,000 and brought up my concerns, including giving them the quote on repairing the basement. I put in an offer at $109,000 and the seller considered himself lucky to get it with the issues brought up on the home inspection, so the offer was accepted.

At this point, my wife and I had moved into the three-family and we had a closing date on the two-family, so I rented a dumpster and was ready to start throwing things out as soon as the paper was signed. I hadn't learned after my first experience that oftentimes the closing doesn't go exactly as planned. I found out the day that we were supposed to close, that we wouldn't be able to close, and here I'd already spent the money on the dumpster and I was so excited and invested in this project.

There was an issue with the city and the title – something wasn't split correctly with the sewer lines. I don't remember exactly, but this was before I had the level of knowledge on real estate that I do now, so I wasn't really paying attention. I just knew that we couldn't close after an entire winter had gone by and I'd already paid for the dumpster. I was really upset that I had the dumpster there and couldn't do anything with it. I'd already taken time off work to go in and rip everything out, cut up the carpets, throw out all the chairs, broken stuff, and debris from all the work I was going to do.

Not doing the work wasn't an option for me, so I took a big risk and asked the sellers if I could go in and do the work prior to the closing. I always tell my clients not to do this, like I was told by my real estate agent and mentor, Jim – it's absolutely crazy! The closing could be canceled altogether and then all the time and money that you put into it will be lost. Fortunately, the best outcome came from it. The sellers agreed to let me start the work and I went to town on that house. I threw out the fridge, cut up all the carpets, demolished some of the stuff that needed to be demolished, and I pulled it all off in just two days by myself. I'd spent about 30 hours in two days in that house, filling up that dumpster, and I didn't even own the house yet. And because I didn't own it, I wasn't allowed to turn the water on to test the heat, despite it being winter out.

Another three months go by and we can't close on this house because of the same title issue amongst other things. Eventually, of course, we did close on it. I was so thankful for that and to finally own the house I'd been waiting for such a long time. Now I had two vacant units, and I needed to get them filled quickly.

We had some contractors come in to replace the roof and fix everything structurally in that regard so that now the house wasn't leaking. We still had the issue with the basement, but I figured the house had been there since the '80s and it hadn't fallen, so it couldn't have been *that* bad. I decided that we'd fix the basement later, but we needed to get the units fixed up first and then get some tenants in there as soon as possible.

From the first two renovations, I learned that it doesn't make sense for me to do all the work, so I had a flooring company come in. I hired a painter and had him come in to paint everything for me for $500 per unit. A good friend of mine, Tim, was one of my tenants and also a licensed electrician, so I had him come through and take care of all the wiring for me. It was the first time I'd ever accepted help that wasn't my family, and I was actually paying professionals to come in and do a project, people who weren't working on the weekends and weren't working at night. While I was at work, my projects were getting done. In two short weeks, I had two fully renovated apartments ready to rent.

What a completely different experience! If I had done it myself, it likely would've taken a month per apartment, as the three-family I renovated myself did.

I have my mentor to thank for this new way of looking at things. If it weren't for Jim, I would have been doing it all myself and lost precious time that I could put toward building what would soon become my empire.

It took only a single month to renovate and find tenants for the two-family, whereas it had taken three months on the two apartments that I'd renovated myself. Another piece that contributed to finding tenants earlier, aside from the apartments being completed faster, is that I had learned from my first few times, and by this point, I was pretty good at time management and finding tenants.

I was getting better at the system. I was starting to figure it out. I was dialing it in.

Of course, this building had a horror story too. I remember telling my wife that we'd spend only about $3,000 a year on the house – at most, we'd spend no more than $10,000. It had already cost us $28,000 down to buy the house, and we had some money saved still. I also had some credit card space if we needed to use it.

She agreed to a maximum of $10,000 and it's hilarious how the Universe works, because we ended up spending exactly that. We spent $3,000 on the top floor apartment, $3,000 on the bottom floor, and the rest went to when we were finally able to turn the water on and the pipes burst everywhere and we were forced to replace the furnace that had blown when we turned it on.

The blowing of the furnace was actually a pretty scary thing if you've never seen it before. I was in the basement with my plumber, now a good friend of mine, and I told him I'd turned the water on and it had worked, so we went to the next furnace. He turned it on and flames shot out at us from the bottom and then sucked back in, like an angry dragon firing a warning shot as a traveler approached his treasure.

I said, "Do you want to try it again? Maybe it was only a fluke, clearing things out or something. Maybe it's still fine."

My buddy was shaking his head and sucking in through his teeth. "Dude, I know this is a big expense for you, but I'm not turning it on. And I will never, ever work for you again if you don't replace this furnace."

After taking some time to consider it and seeing that my friend was serious, I decided to replace the furnace. It was an expense that I hadn't accounted for, but fortunately we had the money sitting right there, so we spent it and finished the rest of the renovations.

Finally, we got the units rented, and things were starting to look fantastic. Rents started coming in and we were profiting. We were living for free in the three-family AND we were pulling a profit! Every single month, the two-family was earning us $800 a month. It fueled me. I realized that if I could cash flow $800 a month on a two-family, then I could cash flow even more on a three-family that I wasn't living in. It was perfect. It was exactly what I was looking for – making money without having to spend 40 or more hours a week in an office. It was my side job, and I wanted to make it my living.

I was thrilled by the idea that instead of us paying $1,500 a month to live, we were now getting paid $800 a month to live and not have to pay rent. Instead of losing $1,500 a month, we were gaining $800 a month on top of saving the $1,500 a month. We were earning $2,300 a month from these two properties.

It was a perfect business, completely different from anything I'd ever experienced. I didn't want to buy a single-family house right now. That was a money pit. I wanted to do this again, to buy another rental property that would pay us for owning it instead of sucking our "money-well" dry, like our first house had.

My wife did not agree...

-Your single-family home is not an investment. It is a liability.

CHAPTER 3

FINANCIAL FREEDOM

So, at this point in the story, the year is 2014. I now own two rental properties – no single-families. I work a fulltime job making $70,000 a year sitting at a desk, typing every so often, teaching Excel classes, and talking to airlines to book travel for different vice presidents at Johnson & Johnson. I literally do nothing at my job and have an easy 20 minute commute with barely any traffic. My wife has quit her job and is running her wedding invitation business, which is making more than her fulltime employment was before.

She's at home enjoying herself, doing graphic design, and I'm helping her build this business. I started reading a lot of books because she and I started seeing success in trying new things, so educating ourselves became even more important than ever. She read "The 4-Hour Workweek," which changed her life. We read "The Four Agreements," another phenomenal book recommended to us by the friend who photographed our wedding and whom we now did a lot of business with in the wedding industry. We were opening our minds, learning more, and realizing that being entrepreneurs is the way to go. We were making more money than we had ever made before, and now we were very close to this mystical thing called "financial freedom".

We're walking our dogs every day together, just talking. We finally booked a vacation to Portugal. Now that the buildings are done, we're in a good spot. Now my two goals are to focus more on my relationship with my wife and this thing called real estate.

I had been listening to a podcast of real estate investors called "Bigger Pockets" every day on my lunch, trying to catch up on the 75 podcasts they had at that time – now they're somewhere past 200. Josh Dorking and Brandon Turner, the hosts, were like my best friends that I'd never met. I listened to them so often that it felt like I'd known them forever.

They talked all the time about going to these things called REIAs – Real Estate Investor Associations. They always said to go out and meet the real estate investors in my neighborhood, so I googled it and found three or four in my area. It was at such an event that my aunt invited me too when I learned for the first time that she owned not one, but two investment properties.

Now I started meeting all these people that owned multies, and had owned them for years, but I didn't know they existed until I started looking for them, for these people who were like me, doing what I was doing. In sales we call it the reticular activator. You buy a Toyota and suddenly Toyota show up on every street you turn down. They've always been there, of course, you just don't realize it until you own it. People notice the things that are important to them, that's how the subconscious mind works.

Anyway, I started meeting all these people, going to all these REIAs and I'll never forget this day, because it was another of those catalysts that made me into the man I am. I sat beside my aunt and a man on stage said, "I've sold 700 houses in my career. I own this. I own that. I flip 60 houses a year. I just bought this house in Cape Cod and" – he pointed his finger into the crowd and, I swear, he was looking directly at me – "if you want to be successful in this business, you need to get your real estate license and become a real estate agent."

I turned to my aunt and said, "I'm going to get my real estate license."

She said, "Oh, you are? Well, you know what, I've been thinking about it. Maybe I should."

I said, "I'm not thinking about it. I'm going to get it because I'm going to be a successful real estate investor. And this man who has done more than anybody I know is saying go get your license. That's the path."

Right around this same time, I finally hit the breaking point at my job. I was a $40,000 a year person making $70,000 a year, plus I had all this rental income coming in, and yet my boss was still laying into me and causing unnecessary stress. I hated it. I remember wondering why I took all the crap from my boss. I had such an easy job, and I remember being frustrated because she was grinding my gears on a project. Looking back this was my financial blueprint snapping back on my like a rubber band. In truth if you want to make more money than you are used too... You first have to become used to more money.

I called my wife and said, "Babe, I'm quitting my job. I'm done."

Our relationship had been rough lately. It was one of the reasons we'd planned the vacation to Portugal. She'd been stressed out with the living situations over the past few months of going through the house sale and buying the two new houses. It's not the life she'd signed up for and she wasn't happy about what I was doing. My own jealousy that she got to be home and I had to work a job I felt no passion for was putting all kinds of stress on me too and it was taking time away from me doing what I really wanted to do. So, me quitting my job was going to allow me to build my business, help her with her business, and allow us to spend more time working on the relationship. I wanted nothing more than to make us work. She was the love of my life, remember.

I hadn't stopped buying houses though, I had a single-family and a three-family under agreement, both on the side of another house I already owned and I had $25,000 saved up. I told my wife, "I don't even care about those houses right now. I just can't be my authentic self if I continue to do this. I'm done. I'm going to be a real estate investor. I'm getting my license to be a real estate agent and that's how I'll make money from now on. I can do this. I know I can. Your business is already making money, and I'll push your business even harder. I'll pick up the phones, I'll make more calls, I'll make more lists, and I'm going to go and pursue this thing called real estate."

My wife told me, "Look, I really don't want you to do that. I really don't want you to quit your job. I just quit my job a few months ago and I don't feel super stable about this. But if you promise me you can do it, if you promise me you're going to make sure we don't suffer at all, then do whatever you want and we'll figure it out."

That was all I needed. I went to human resources and told them I was done. I never walked back into that building as an employee. I've gone back many times now to get referrals from my friends, but never again as an employee. It was a freeing day but it was also terrifying, because there was no going back for me. I knew in that moment I was never, ever going to work for a W2 at somebody else's business ever again. I was going to be my own boss from now on.

It was freeing.

It was terrifying.

I wasn't sure how to become a real estate agent, so I called up good friend and mentor – you remember Jim. It was funny, actually. Imagine calling somebody up and asking them how you can take their job. Well, when I look back at it, that's basically what I did. I called up my real estate agent and said, "Jim, how do I get my real estate license? I went to this event and this guy was saying to be a successful real estate investor, I need to get my real estate license. He was talking about investing and all these investors who buy with no money down, or with seller financing and all these other awesome options."

Jim said, "Gualter, Gualter. All right. Ease up. Yes, I can show you the way to get your real estate license. But then I'm losing my best client. I mean, you've already bought three houses and you're talking about buying another one every year, maybe more as you progress. I'm going to be losing my best client."

I told him, "Yeah, I get it, Jim. I'll still send you referrals. I just want to get my real estate license to have MLS access and save money on my own purchases. Little things."

Eventually, Jim said, "You know what? I really like you. You're a good guy. I'm thankful for the houses that I've been able to work on for you, and I'm thankful for all the referrals you've sent me. You've given me a lot of business. Let's get you your real estate license."

I guess every good thing has its end, but with the end of that good thing, it opens an opportunity for something better. Jim mentored me, trained me, and gave me the courses. For the next couple months, I studied real estate and got my test scheduled a month out because they were so busy at the time, they couldn't take me.

During that waiting period, my wife and I went on a trip to Portugal, where she asked me for a divorce. She'd asked for a divorce before, but I'd been able to talk her out of it with the Portugal trip. "We're really stressed out right now, babe. We've been working so hard on our new life. What we need is a vacation to reenergize our relationship. Let's do this trip and see if we can make it work."

This next chapter is not going to be easy for me.

-Don't quit your job until you have created enough passive income to more than support you.

CHAPTER 4

DIVORCE & BETRAYAL

This part of my life is something I try my hardest to avoid talking about, but for the sake of this book and for the sake of the people who have, are, or might someday go through it, I'm going to share this with you. I only talk about this now because I believe it will benefit others to see that it's possible to go through these things and still come out okay on the other side, better in fact. Understand that I seek no sympathy in telling this part of my story, because honestly, my life is amazing now. I share this in the interest of coming out genuine and honest. It was the worst time in my life that I can remember. My heart was ripped out of my chest, and I was falling apart. I was at a point where I was absolutely certain things weren't going to work out.

I'm here despite all that, and I'm thankful for all the experiences I went through that built me into the man I am today.

So, here goes.

My wife and I were not doing well (it goes without saying). For the past year, she had been trying to get out of the relationship, and at the same time, I was very headstrong. I didn't listen well. I was young and thought I knew everything. I knew we had issues, so I came up with all kinds of plans to fix them and I laid it out for her, "Look, we're having this issue and this is the solution, so we're just going to do it and everything will be good again."

I thought I was invincible. I thought I could handle the whole world, and if things weren't coming out my way, all I needed to do was put in more energy and effort. I didn't listen. I tried to fix it without knowing the extent of the trouble. In sales I make sure my students understand, it's all about listening. I'm very good at sales now. I'm a very good listener now. That's probably the biggest lesson I learned from my relationship – if you don't listen enough, eventually the other person will just get tired of hearing you talk and walk away.

Well, I wasn't listening to her. Before the trip to Portugal, she asked for a divorce, so I booked the trip in hopes of fixing things by getting rid of some stress. Then, when we got back, she asked me again for a divorce, saying that the trip didn't change anything and that she still wasn't interested in making things work.

Our trip was in August. I'd started working out in July. My wife used to always complain that I wasn't in shape. Maybe, I thought, if I had a better physique, she'd want to stay, or maybe I was subconsciously preparing to be single because I knew I couldn't save us. I honestly can't say. Maybe it was a bit of both.

My cousin started taking me to the gym and training me, teaching me the ins and outs of developing muscle and the physique that I wanted. I became obsessed with working out to the point where that's all I would talk about – I've always loved sharing the things I've learned with others. I was so thankful to have my cousin taking care of me, helping me build my body up, and helping me save my marriage though I hadn't said anything to him about it.

Eventually, I started bringing my wife with me because I thought that might be another way for us to bond and hopefully sway her more in the direction of wanting to make things work.

After about eight weeks of working out, I was really starting to build some muscle and get in great shape. It was to the point where I would see my friends and family – that I hadn't been making time for because I was working on my marriage – and their mouths would drop because of how much muscle I had put on since they'd last seen me almost two months earlier.

Seeing how quickly I'd made progress building up my body, I realized I could do the same thing with making money. I was already doing it with my wife's business and I was ready to start hammering on my own. We had so much free time now that we were both running our own businesses and didn't have to answer to anybody.

We went to the beach all the time, sometimes two or three times a week, in the middle of the day, when nobody was there. We'd just enjoy ourselves. We were making more money than we'd ever made and we had all this free time. It was almost as if we were in an early retirement, only 28 and living this work from home lifestyle, able to work absolutely anywhere we wanted in the world – at home, in Portugal, at a café, at a beach, anywhere.

It didn't matter. She still wasn't happy…

She was constantly asking for a divorce now. She'd get frustrated with me: "I just don't want to be with you anymore."

It was heart-wrenching. I couldn't figure it out. One day, she asked me if I had ever wanted to sleep with anybody else after we'd gotten married, and I told her utterly honestly that I'd never even considered it. I loved her more than anything and she was the only person in the world I ever wanted.

When I asked her, though, she'd said yes. She did want to.

One day – I'm not proud of this, but it's what happened and I've committed to being honest in this book – she'd left her cell phone on the bathroom sink, face down, and it went off. I picked it up and started reading, seeing all these messages from an unsaved number saying things like, "I can't help the way I feel about you," and all this other stuff. I couldn't believe what was going on.

I confronted her about it and I couldn't believe who it was. My cousin, my friend who I'd been going to the gym with, who'd been training both my wife and I. It turned out they'd developed feelings for one another at some point during our gym training.

I couldn't swallow that. My wife was in love with my cousin, who was my new mentor in the gym, the guy who'd taught everything gym-related, the guy who I'd hoped could help me fix my relationship by helping me get the body that my wife wanted me to have. To this day, I still quote him on the things he taught me. Do I hate him? No. Do I hate what he did? Maybe a little, but it's ultimately led me to a much happier place in my life.

When I found everything out, I did what any man who thought he had all the answers would do. I recognized things couldn't work the way they were, but I still wanted them to, so I made one final effort, putting in the last of the energy I had after all the details of their betrayal had worn me down.

I asked her, "Can we salvage our relationship?"

She said, "No."

I asked her, "Can we try marriage counseling?"

She said, "No."

I asked her, "Why?"

She said, "I'm just not interested in fixing it. I've tried so hard. I've worked on it so much."

She said all these things about how hard she's been working at making things work, and here I am just finding out. I'd had no idea how serious things were, because I wasn't listening. I don't doubt that she told me, but I didn't hear what she was *saying*.

Finally, I did what I've never done before—I gave up. It wasn't going to work out. I was willing to do anything, but she wasn't, and if she didn't want it to work, there was no way it could. I went and I filed the paperwork. Originally she wanted a separation, which I filed on September 11, 2014 on our third-year anniversary. But I told her, "A separation isn't going to cut it." I knew I was on a path to accumulating more wealth, and if she wasn't willing to work at our relationship, I wasn't taking any risks. I told her, "If we were doing this, it has to be a divorce. If things work out, they work out."

Four years later, we haven't gotten back together. They did not work out.

The first year, I'd tried reaching out to her once in a while to see if things were going well, but she only lashed out in anger, telling me that I couldn't contact her. I stopped.

We were both surprised by how big a process divorce was. We had to split up our properties, our businesses, our bank accounts, 401k's – it's a big deal. She and I verbally agreed what we were going to do and decided that neither of us needed an attorney. The houses were mine – she didn't want them. I was relieved about that after all the money and work I'd put into them. I was going to pay her back the money that she'd put into the houses. The wedding invitation business was going to be hers and I'd have no part in it. We had a mediator work out all the details. Ultimately, it was a pretty clean deal with very little animosity, all things considered.

Against everybody's advice, I moved out because I was the bigger man, and I was either going to kill her or she was going to kill me. We just couldn't be civil together. At this point, my dad had moved in with his girlfriend and my brother had moved into my dad's old apartment, so I asked my brother if I could come live with him for a while, just until the divorce was finished. He took me in without a question.

When we got to court, she showed up with an attorney anyway and the attorney said, "She's not going to pay you rent," and I couldn't argue. I didn't have an attorney of my own and I didn't know how things worked, so I ended up now not being able to rent that apartment, and only having an income of $800 per month that I was making on the other building. I'd literally just gotten my real estate license in the middle of all this going on, and I'd just quit my job months earlier. I went from living on top of the world to suddenly having nothing – absolutely nothing.

We did the math and determined that I owed her $25,000. Unfortunately, my bank account was down to $10,000. That's all I had left, and I wasn't making any substantial income. If I didn't pay her, she was going to keep one of my houses. She was going to force me to sell one of my houses. Real estate was my business. It was my passion. It was what I was put on this earth to do, and she was taking that away from me.

Well, I wasn't going to let her.

For the second time in my life, I had to humble myself and go to my family.

First, I went to my brother. I texted him: *"Josh, do you mind if I borrow $5,000?"*

I'll never forget his response. I didn't tell him what it was for. I just asked for five grand with no explanation and his response was simple: *"Sure, bro."*

That was it.

I thanked him and after five or six more texts back and forth where we worked out the details of how he should get me the money, he finally said, *"So, should I ask what this is for?"*

When I responded that it was for the divorce, he called me immediately. "DIVORCE?"

"Yeah."

"I thought you guys were just separating."

"Nope. It wasn't going to work, so we're just... divorcing."

I've never heard my brother sound as serious as he did when he said his next words: "Walter, if I ever have anything that you need, it's always going to be yours."

I tried laughing it off to keep myself from tears, but he pressed on.

"I'm dead serious. Those aren't just words. If you need it, it's yours. Whatever it is."

I acknowledged it somberly and told him the same, anything I could do, if it was within my power, I would do for him. There was too much emotion in that moment, so I had to break the tension with a joke, "I can't believe I asked you for five grands and you didn't even blink about it."

"Yeah, well, I'll do anything for the people I love."

That day, I vowed that after I paid him back the money he'd lent me, I would pay him back a hundred fold by helping him make his dreams come true. And I keep my promises.

Unfortunately, that only helped me get up to $15,000 and I still needed another $10,000 to pay her, so I reached out to my father next. I called and said the same thing I did to my brother: "Dad, do you mind if I borrow $10,000? I'll pay you back."

"Absolutely, son. Whatever you need."

My dad was so supportive with this. He'd gone through a much less amicable divorce with my mother, so he wanted to make sure I wasn't alone in this. He came to court with me both times and made sure I was the man he'd raised me to be when I was in the courtroom. I got stressed out and angry in those courtroom sessions when my wife or her attorney said something stupid or did something unexpected, but my father was there and he was my rock. His presence ensured that I was a good, genuine person while I was there and that I didn't rise to my anger. I didn't say anything dumb that I would later regret. He helped me to stay calm as we went through the transaction.

I ended up paying her the money and being left with nothing in my bank account, owing my family $15,000, and having $10,000 of credit card debt. I literally walked out of that courtroom feeling like I was worth less than I was when God put me on this planet – I was worth negative $25,000 and it was terrifying.

I hadn't had *no* money since I was thirteen, but I knew I would find a way. I had my family at my back, I had a work ethic like forged by my father, and I had a real estate license. I was going to figure this game out. Even though I'd never had a sale and had no idea what I was doing, I knew that every single time I worked a job, I figured it out within six months and that I always became the best at what I did. Real estate, I knew, would be the exact same.

I studied every day, watching the pros on YouTube, like Buffini, Ferry, Hopkins and all the other mentors who never knew they were mine. My broker at the time was the local RE/MAX, and I would go to my broker and say, "Hey, what is it you want me to study? What do you want me to do?" He offered these classes and I took every single class and read every single book. An opportunity to study in Boston would come up, so I would go to Boston. My mentor would take me to all these different offices, explaining that they would all try to recruit me, but they'd give me free training in the process, so I went to as many as I could.

My mentor took me to auctions and I asked him a hundred questions about auctions. He took me on appointments and I asked him a hundred questions about what to do and what not to do. I told him I wanted to live a day in his life, and so I shadowed him everywhere. I listened to him as he took calls in the car, paying attention to the words he used and the tone of voice and how they changed based on the client, and I took notes, studying and spending all my time going to the gym and learning real estate.

Every time I went to the gym, I would see my ex-wife there with my cousin, and I would be over here training all by myself like a loser, while they trained on the other side of the gym together. There was a guy at the gym who saw me, and he knew the situation because he was friends with my cousin, and he took me under his wing. He told me that I was either going to train with him or I wasn't training at that gym anymore, because seeing my ex-wife with my cousin was going to mess me up. I told him I was in and we started training at 4:30 in the morning. That meant I had the rest of the day to work on real estate. I left there, showered, then hit the office bright and early.

I asked everybody in that real estate office so many questions that part of me was worried I was annoying them, but it turned out that they loved being asked all those questions. They loved that I valued their knowledge and wanted to learn from them. I found out who were the best agents in the office and I asked to go on appointments with them. Anytime somebody had an open house, I asked if I could go with them or just do it for them. Agents hated doing open houses, but I was doing three or four open houses every single Saturday and Sunday.

I didn't have clients because I was new to real estate, so open houses were the only way I knew how to get business. I'd never worked with anybody before, so I couldn't work off of referrals. I spent my days studying real estate, sales, hitting the gym, and talking to as many people as I possibly could about real estate. It was stressful and it was scary and I just kept pushing.

Eventually, I figured it out. I sucked at sales. I made a whopping $17,000 in my first year in real estate, which was nowhere near enough to cover my bills. Fortunately, my brother was letting my live practically rent-free at his place. I lived there for a whole year. He really proved that he meant what he'd said about giving me anything he could, and every day I woke up in his apartment, I solidified my vow to myself that I would make his dreams come true.

Without my brother, I don't know that I'd be where I am today. While I was living with him, I'd constantly get emails from recruiters telling me, "Citizens Bank is offering you $25 an hour," or "We just want you to come back to Johnson & Johnson. How's $35 an hour sound?" or "Coca Cola will hire you for $30 an hour."

I don't know how many times I went to my brother said, "Hey, I'm being offered this job making good money. Should I take it? I know I can make this real estate thing work, but I'm terrified. I'm scared I'm not going to be able to do it fast enough. I'm already in a bunch of credit card debt and I'm just racking up more every day. I feel bad because I'm living in your house and I'm barely contributing financially. I know I can make real estate work, and I really don't want to go back to a nine-to-five. If I do, I know I'm not going to push real estate the way I want to. I only have a certain amount of energy and I don't want to waste it."

My brother looked me in the eye and he said, "Gualter, you always become the best at everything you do. You're going to make this real estate thing work. If you get anymore emails from recruiters, delete them right away. Don't read them. Don't even open them. You've got this on lock. You're going to make this work because that's what you do."

I still get chills when I think about that day, when I think about that conversation. He knew. He knew what I was capable of before I knew it. I listened to him. Anytime I got an email from a recruiter, I remembered his words: "Don't read them. Don't even open them. You've got this on lock. You're going to make this work because that's what you do." So I did delete them, and I kept doing what I knew how to, working hard, working hard, working hard, and whenever I doubted myself, I reminded myself that I owed my brother his dream and I owed myself mine.

No matter what happened in that first year, he encouraged me and I pushed through. I got a bad tenant I had to evict because they weren't paying rent, and I pushed through, losing money. My transmission blew on my truck I'd owned for ten years, and I pushed through, putting another $2,000 on my credit cards. I started spending money on marketing, and my credit cards fast approached $20,000 in debt. I looked at it every month and put the minimum payments every time. It was going to end. Soon, all the hard work was going to pay off and this terrifying time of being broke was going to end. There were dark times where I didn't think I had the energy to push through, to make this work, but my brother had faith in me and I couldn't let him down. I owed him his dream, and I owed myself mine. I kept pushing.

In December of my first year of real estate, after being at RE/MAX for almost a year, I got a phone call from Cameron Real Estate Group's recruiter, Nicole Johnson. The call came while I was listening to Bigger Pockets and they said to get into real estate, work for an investment company, work for a property management company, work for somebody who's doing what I wanted to do. Nicole called me and said, "Cameron Real Estate Group is the biggest real estate investors in Boson. We're going to send you on seller appointments. We're going to send you out to be the investor first, then an agent second." The commission split was higher and there was more training and all these different ways to make money, but the only part that mattered was that they were the best investors in Boston, the best in Massachusetts.

I told her, "Nicole, I'm on my way. I'll do it. Sign me up."

She said, "Oh, we're an hour and a half away in Wakefield."

I hesitated a minute and then shook my head. "It doesn't matter. I'm probably never going to come to the office, but sign me up."

That call, that decision, has made all the difference. I'm grateful for the opportunity to work with such amazing people, like Tommy Cafarella, Bill Mandell, and Bob DeVito. These guys were literally the best in the industry and if it weren't for that call, if it weren't for me being open and able to take that opportunity, I don't know where I would be today.

-When you think you are listening, stop and listen.

CHAPTER 5

THE YEAR OF THE COMEBACK

The first portion of this book describes how I reached the lowest point in my life, where I'd lost everything and had to start again from less than nothing. This second half, though, is all about the growth mindset, changing the past and how things worked previously, deciding that I'm not going to deal with being broke anymore.

After everything that happened, I decided to take a good hard look at myself. I wanted something bigger and better in my life and I realized that I was the only static, unchanging thing in my life. I knew that if I wanted my life to be different, I had to change the way I looked at the world and the way I interacted with it. I had some great mentors both in real life and in the written word that helped me become the man I am today – the man I've always wanted to be.

Probably the biggest change I made was the voracity with which I approached continuing education. The previous year, when I thought I'd been killing it, I was reading roughly a book a month. One day, I heard Grant Cardone say, "If you want a 52-to-1 advantage, read a book a week." Crazy as it sounded, I decided to take on the challenge.

He calls it the 52-to-1 advantage because the average American reads only one book a year, and usually they don't even finish it. The theory, then, is that if you buy books that are going to help you grow, books that will expand your knowledge, and you read one of those a week, not only will you be more capable of responding to mental challenges, deducing logic, and understanding complex subject matter, but you will become more aware of the situations that most people are blind to.

Reading a book a week is better than any college degree. It will literally change your life.

I looked for any book that had the word "millionaire" or "rich" in the title and I read as many as I could as quickly as I could. Anything that mentioned financial improvement or success, I'd grab those titles and burn through them. Bigger Pockets had a list of the top five books for success, so I read those and I started asking anybody I met that was more successful than I, "What are the top five books?" My own top five are listed at the end of this book.

The year 2015 was tough for me – I'd lost my marriage, I'd lost money, I'd left my job, I'd been trying to figure out who I was, who I wanted to be, I'd been hitting the gym, learning sales, learning business and mostly learning who I was. Despite all the tough times I had in 2015, it primed me for my comeback in 2016. I came into the new year, digging for knowledge like I'd never dug for it before, like a starving animal bursting out of its cage and consuming everything in its path. I sold 19 houses in 2016 for a total of $90,000. That's nearly a 530% increase over the last year, where I'd made only $17,000, claiming only $12,000 on my taxes after expenses. Ninety thousand dollars just from my real estate business, and I still made $25,000 off my rental properties as well.

All of this was thanks to changing my mindset and the tenacity with which I approached the work. I'd figured out the game: If I wanted to change my income, I had to change myself first. A lot of that came from the Millionaire Mind Intensives put on by T. Hary Eker and Peaks Potential which later became Success Resources. This is that kind of event where you get together with a bunch of strangers in a hotel room and learn about the secrets to building wealth and attracting money. I went to two of them, one at the end of 2015 and the other in mid-2016. They changed my life and put me in the right mindset for success. I set my goal at making $100,000 in 2016, and nothing was going to stop me. In the end, I hit $115,000, though after taxes I only took home $86,000. Still, it was the mindset that changed and that's what allowed me to make $100,000. It wasn't an option to not make it.

Fortunately, even though I'd lost all that money in the divorce, 2016 was a great year in real estate. Fortunately the two family house I owned went up in value quite a bit and after having held it for so long, the bank allowed me to refinance it to a cash out refi. This is another moment where my family came to save me – my brother put his name on the loan for me since I didn't have the W2 income to do it myself at the time. So, with that cash payout, I paid off my dad and my brother easily.

Oh, and that dream I'd promised my brother? Yeah, I got to lend him $15,000 of the $50,000 he invested to open his own tremendously successful business, a ninja warrior and parkour school called AMP Academy LLC. I'm so proud of him and everything he does. If you ever have the opportunity, the original location is in Fall River, MA, since we both made a promise to make our city a better place – I'm doing it with real estate, and my brother is doing it by encouraging the youth and teaching them emotional and psychological strength all while having fun with physical activities.

He's got plans to pop these locations up all over the country to help children everywhere and to give adults a place to get fit the fun way, by playing, instead of trudging along to a gym that they might not fully enjoy. AMP Academy is really a phenomenal place and it's a blessing that I'm able to be a part of it. You can check out his progress by visiting: ampacademygym.com. Seeing how far he's come with it and how many lives he's affected is absolutely amazing. You see, real estate is what allowed me to help him fund that business, his dream. He put in two thirds, but a third of that came from refinancing one of my properties.

Along with contributing to his opening that business, I was able to use that money to buy another three houses that year. I'd gone all of 2015 without buying a single house, but in 2016 I bought three. In the next few chapters, I'll explain how I was able to do that and all the steps that were involved in closing those deals.

As if buying three houses in a single year wasn't enough, I set up my own real estate team and built us an office. One of the buildings that I'd bought ended up having a great space for a storefront, but it was me alone in July of 2016 when I took the initiative to tell my broker Tom what I wanted to do. I wanted to open an Fall River location under the Cameron Real Estate Group's name.

I'm blessed to have such an amazing broker. Tom told me, "You should. I trust you. You're going to do it with or without me." And he was right. Tom hadn't known me for very long, but he had known me long enough to know that I was going to make my life exactly what I wanted it to be one way or the other. He gave me his approval, his support, coaching and became my next Mentor. In only a year's time, my office was up to nearly 25 agents, and still growing – always growing.

In August of 2016, I'd already closed $70k in commissions and I was exhausted. The new agents that I'd brought in by that time were catching on fast and beginning to close deals themselves and started taking my leads. Things were starting to move fast and at this point it was important for me to figure out exactly what I wanted in life, so I took two months off from transactions allowing the team to run all of my leads so I could focus on fleshing out my goals.

So many people are shocked when I tell them that I decided to take two months off, but that's because they don't realize that by August, I'd already made $70,000, which was almost double the speed that it used to take me, and almost double what I really needed to live. After making in only eight months what it used to take me a year to make, I went through another mindset shift. At that point, it wasn't about the money anymore. Now pay attention. I share my dollar amounts with you at the risk of and awareness that this was 2016. The dollar values will change over time and I grew up in Fall River a city where $25,000 was the average income. Depending on where you grew up economically these dollar amounts will be perceived differently. It is the percentages of growth that are important.

I asked myself the following questions: How did I want to live my life? What is it I wanted to do in life? What do I want that will get me up in the morning? Who was I? What did I enjoy doing? What was my passion? For two months, I didn't want to close any more deals. I was all set with making money, but I still had friends and family reaching out to me because they wanted to buy houses.

They were still calling me and texting me, saying, "Hey, can you help me buy a house?" or "Can you sell my house for me?" I got to a point where I realized there was no getting out of this business that I started, and that's when it hit me that it wasn't about me. It wasn't about making money. People still needed me. My friends and family needed the knowledge and skill-sets I had picked up. I wanted my financial freedom, to never have to work another day in my life, but I was still a cog in the wheel. They needed me to go out there and help them. So, what could I do?

My solution was to build a team of experts in the field of real estate, to train them to do everything with the same passion and ethics that I myself always helped any past, present, or future homeowner. By training a team of people who could do everything that I had been promoting, I could help my team financially, and I could help countless multiples of people. By myself, I could only help maybe 30 people a year, but by training a team of 25 people to help the same way I do, I could help exponentially more people.

I could continue helping people but at exponential rates, and using far less of my time, allowing me the freedom to continue and grow and do all the other things that I enjoy doing, like reading books and learning and teaching. I started out by bringing three agents on and training them. At this point, they were some of the top agents in the office. I taught the team the science behind the selfie, trained them to take video for social media, gave them titles like Louise Methot, "the condo queen", and taught them to end everything with our tag line, "When you have a choice, Always work with the Best". There are more and more rock-stars who've joined the team as well as participated in my Agent Alchemist training programs, Bootcamps, Intensives, Summit events and Masterminds since, who are a part of our continually growing tribe as well. To learn more about my training programs and events you can go to AgentAlchemist.com to see what is new and coming up.

Opening the office was a huge step for me, and it was scary in the begining. I was renting an apartment at the time and I didn't have the money for such a project. It was the office or a place to live, or secret option number three – **there's always a secret option number three** – get rid of the apartment, set up the office, and move into the tiny little 6' x 13' room in the back of my new office, which had been listed as a walk-in closet (since it had no closet itself and therefore wasn't a bedroom) when I bought the house.

It should come as no surprise to you that I'm willing to do W.I.T, whatever it takes to achieve success, so I moved into the little room with a small cot and a dresser. I put up a shower curtain to use as a closet for my clothes. I had my bookshelf and all my books, and I had my audiobooks. By day, I was crushing appointments – appointment to appointment to appointment, back to back to back – and then at night, I'd get into my tiny room, close my door, and read.

Whether reading or listening to an audiobook, I sat and made notes. I'd write down everything I was doing right and everything I was doing wrong, analyzing, looking for how I could make myself better at what I did and how I could keep my business growing. Any time I went to an appointment and things didn't work out, I'd write it down. I'd look for why it didn't work out. What had I done wrong? More importantly, though, when I had an appointment that *did* work out, I'd write down what I'd done that made it successful.

It was all very fascinating to me, trying to understand how I was able to connect with each person and create value. By this time, I was dating somebody new, and my girlfriend was very supportive. She had actually moved to Fall River from Las Vegas, and so we would fly out to Vegas to visit her family, and I finally began to see the world from her point of view. Out in Vegas, things are completely different. The way people did things, the way they thought, was so vastly different from how I was doing things back home. I saw all this luxury, all this money that I'd never been exposed to growing up in such a depressed city. I saw people driving around in all these crazy expensive cars and I saw luxury apartments, and I felt my mindset begin to shift again. I started to realize that there's more to the world than the little box I'd grown up in. It was all thanks to being open to new experiences and traveling away from where I had spent my whole life.

Despite her having lived in luxury for so long, she was so supportive of me when I was struggling to make my office grow. I had opened the office and was hiring these new agents, training them, and all the while, nobody knew that I lived in the tiny little box of a room across the hall from my office. My working space was actually larger than my living space. There was thin hollow door with a lock separating my perceived success from my shameful living situation.

It was very difficult for my pride, but I'd still go out in the city, dressed to impress, shaking hands and kissing babies, taking videos, taking selfies, and telling everybody that I was the best, at this game. That they should work with me, because after all "When you have a choice, Always work with the Best." "I'm the Best." "Come work with me and I'll make you the best real estate agent in the city." And then I'd go home to my office, turn the key to the thin hollow door and regroup my emotional energy and remind myself that this was temporary.

I'd be having my meetings, teaching my team how to crank up their sales and be amazing at what they do, and in the back of my head I was thinking, "Wow. I live about eight feet away behind that thin hollow door with a lock. I actually shower here in this office, and nobody knows." It was a difficult thing. I remember sitting on my cot one night and reminding myself over and over again, "This is temporary. It's not going to be like this forever. And when this is all done, I will never, ever, ever have to do this again. I'm never going to come back to this place where I'm forced to live so uncomfortably and I'm going to do whatever it takes to be successful. And when I get there, I'm going to teach people how to do the same thing, so they can get out of those scary uncomfortable places in their lives."

I don't live in that tiny room anymore, and I haven't for a long time. The next chapter is going to be fun, because I'll be talking about some of the properties I bought and some of the projects we've done, and when I remember sitting in that tiny room and promising all those things to myself, it's crazy to see where I am now. I had bought 12 houses at the time of this first publishing – most people only ever buy one – and every single one of the buildings I own pays me rent.

Because I can bring this experience to my students. They know exactly how it's going to be, and if something goes wrong, they know exactly how to fix it, because I've been in that situation before. They know how stressful it is to buy a property, or to own and sell one. I make it a priority to teach my students, real estate teams, agents, investors to always relate to any situation for their clients and the people they come in contact with. In life your pain will one day become your power, which you will use to help the people you work with.

-Have a positive mindset and seek the things you want.

CHAPTER 6

A LESSON LEARNED

House number five was one of the weirdest deals I've done to this day. I used to get all these leads from Tom, and I would go on the appointments. Most of the appointments were about forty-five minutes away in Brockton, Quincy, Milford or other places, but occasionally he'd give me one from my city, which I always loved because they were right in my backyard.

I pulled up to the house on the south end of Fall River, where I grew up, next to a convenience store. I'd driven by this place about a thousand times and when I pulled up this time, I thought the same thing I always had, "Boy, this is a terrible location." It was a tiny house right next door from a convenience store, had no parking, and had people sitting on their porch across the street, smoking and drinking. It's a mess.

Despite that, after a short struggle to open the gate, I walked up the house, and knocked. The sweetest little old lady on planet Earth opened the door and invited me in. The house was packed, like Hoarders-style packed, stuff everywhere, and more cats than any one person should have. The whole thing looked like it was straight out of a movie. Like I said, she was super sweet, but she also had some strange characters in the house. I think they were homeless people she used to help or merely people who would come by and she would feed them and give them a placed to sleep if they needed it.

After walking through the house with her, at Tom's request, I decided to make an offer for $66,000, which I knew was lower than she wanted, and she declined. The truth was, it wasn't really worth much more than that. I ended up listing it for her at $100,000, got the paperwork signed, strapped the sign up on her gate, and drove away.

The next day, I got a call from the same lady and she said, "I have to get out of this house. Can your boss bring up his offer to $77,000? That would allow me enough to move." She apparently owed $75,000, but she wanted out of the responsibility of owning the property.

So, I called up Tom and said, "Hey, brother. What do you think? She's asking us to come up more than $10,000. What's the move on this?

After some discussion, Tom told me, "Unfortunately, it doesn't make sense."

I agreed with him. With all the renovations that needed to be done, $77,000 was a really bad deal. I explained that to her and apologized, assuring her that it was on the market and I was going to try my best to sell it.

She thought about it and then asked me, "What about you? I know you buy houses. What could I do so that you'd buy it?"

I thought about it for a few moments and finally told her, "Look, I'm financed out right now. I don't have the income to do my own financing. Honestly, the only thing that I could do is if I took over your mortgage, then I could finance it and give you the $2,000 you need in cash."

And she said yes.

That terrified me, because I didn't want this house. If Tom wasn't willing to buy it at that price, I already knew it wasn't a great deal, but I figured worst case scenario that I could still rent it out and eventually the market would come back to a point where I could sell it to get out from under it. The way I was looking at it, if I rented it out for $900 per month without making any renovations to it, I'd make $100 per month. Basically, I'd spend $2,000 and walk away with a new rental property.

Still, I was iffy, and she wanted to talk about it with her son to see if things would work. To me, that was a relief – I thought I'd have a way out. I figured I could talk to the son, explain how it all worked, and her son would see reason and tell his mom that it was too much risk for her and that it didn't make sense to do.

We set up the appointment for me to meet with her and her son the very next day. I explained everything in no uncertain terms. I said, "Look, she's on the hook. If I don't pay, it doesn't affect me at all. It affects her credit." I was trying to scare them out of the deal.

It didn't work.

They all agreed that it made the most sense for her to do the deal that I was trying so hard to get out of. I should have walked away then and there, but I kept trying to convince myself that I could make it work. The place was a dump and there were a lot of issues, but there was also a new heating system and it didn't seem like there was a lot of damage.

I ended up going through with the deal, despite my hesitation and against my better judgment. My attorney was phenomenal and went through everything to make sure I was as protected as possible in this deal. When the deal was finished, she got out and I was surprised at how well she'd cleared out all the junk that had been piling up. But as I looked around the now empty house, that's when I started noticing the big holes that rats had been using to get into the house, chewing their way through everything. There were thick layers of cat fur clumped up around the radiators, and the roof started leaking. Right off the bat, replacing the roof cost me $4,000 and I winced.

Now that the previous owners clutter was out of the house, I noticed that the floor in the kitchen was sagging and had so much bounce to it I felt like I was on a trampoline. My contractor ended up ripping out one of the cabinets and pulling up about ten feet of the floor only to find that the sills were all rotted out in that corner – and I mean completely rotted out, wasted away, gone! It ended up costing me another $2,000 to repair the floor's structure, add new flooring, put new stucco on the walls, and everything else that came with that. We did it as inexpensively as possible, while making sure that it was done safely, reusing pieces and shifting things around, but it was way more than I expected to spend on this house.

By the end of all the repairs to make it livable, I'd already put in an extra $10,000 into this house that was already a bad purchase. I'm in $87,000 at this point, and I still owe my broker money for letting me take that deal from him.

Finally, I was able to get a tenant in there, and within only two months, the tenants were having issues with the heating bill. He hadn't even received the heating bill yet, but he was upset about how cold it was in there. It turns out that this same tenant was suing his last landlord and at that point I finally decided, "You know what? I don't want to have a tenant here. I do need to sell this thing." So, I evicted the tenant and put the house on the market in the dead of winter for $140,000. Naturally, it didn't sell. I dropped it to $130,000, then $120,000, then to $110,000, and finally to $100,000, and it still wasn't moving.

At one point, I'd gotten somebody in and had them under agreement until the home inspector came in. Before the inspector even finished, the buyer saw the neighbors sitting on their porch and decided they weren't interested in living there, so I had to put it back on the market for $99,000, and it still wasn't moving, through the winter and through the spring, and I still sat on this property.

One day I got a call from one of my neighbors saying that there have been people living in the house. I thought, "That's impossible, "but I went over with the police and found that a homeless man had been living on the property. He was removed and I locked the house really tight again, replacing all the locks. The next day, I got another call about somebody else in there. Turns out they'd broken a window and busted a bunch of the pipes under the sink trying to steal the copper. Mice had gotten back in again, so I had to do another mouse treatment. The house became a real issue. It had gone from not making me money to becoming a headache almost overnight.

I spent more money on the property, fixing windows, replacing locks, repairing pipes. I decided that since it wasn't selling, I'd have to rent it again, but I decided to do a lease option to purchase. I resolved to rent to somebody who wanted to buy the property and was able to find this really great guy to put in there. He was a little bit of a headache at first, because he wanted everything fixed perfectly.

It was cool being able to say I owned the house, but I still wished I hadn't bought it. The person I bought it from had needed out of it, though. She and I are still friends – she's on my Facebook every day saying hi and thanks. Me taking the house saved her life, she said, because she gets to live a much better quality life now. She was on a very small fixed income and getting out of that property meant that she was able to get

Section 8 housing, leaving her with enough money for food and her normal expenses without falling behind on her bills. The way I look at it now is that I did her a favor. I suffered a lot for it, and I also learned a lot of lessons from the property, but I lost more money than I made on it. Eventually, I did to put it back on the market, and sold if for $97,000 and broke even after commissions and maintenance over the 3 year I held it. The market had improved enough to where I could get out from under it, but I will always remember the many lessons I learned from this deal.

The main lesson I learned here is that sometimes even at a great price, is not a great deal. Even when the prices are low, location is still extremely important and I've learned to pay much more attention to that. Sometimes even the best can make mistakes, but it's all about how we come back from those that matters.

-Price is Relative

-Never buy on a main street

-Never buy a house without a basement

CHAPTER 7

ONE LAST HURDLE

Now that you've heard about my worst deal, let me tell you about my best deal. It was my third purchase in 2016 and my fifth property overall and it was an absolute dream. I was able to purchase this four-family for only $150,000 and it cash flowed nearly $1,500 every month after expenses. I did have a Section 8 tenant in there when I purchased it, which I was worried about, but they're still there today and they're a great tenant, paying rent on time and they might even be one of my best tenants.

While this deal was hands-down my best deal, it was also one of my more complicated ones, and it took me almost as long as my first three-family. This one went under agreement somewhere around January and it got pushed back month after month after month and I didn't close on it until August, which held up a lot of other plans.

See, I had the single-family going, I had this four-family going, and I was working on closing the three-family storefront. I figured I would close the three, then close the single, and then a few months later I would close the four, then using all cash flow and equity, I'd go and buy this big six-family that I'd been looking at. Unfortunately, the four-family kept pushing back, month after month, not closing.

I was forced to back out of the six-family deal. I couldn't back out of the single-family deal – although in retrospect, maybe I should have – because despite it being a terrible deal for me, it seemed so easy. It was $2,000 out of pocket, then I'd have a house. Easy. Quick. So, since it was the easiest deal (even though it ended up being the worst in every other way) I decided I wasn't going to back out of that one. Still, at the time, I knew that every time I got up to two or three deals at the same time, it was too much for me to juggle.

I was getting to the point where I had three deals under agreement and I knew putting a fourth under was going to be a bad idea. The six-family was going to be the biggest cash flow deal at a purchase price of $170,000, but it was on the other side of the city, had no parking, and needed lots of renovations to get it up and running. There were a lot of tenants that would've needed to be evicted and I didn't know if I had the cash flow or the reserves to get through such a massive renovation. For the down-payment, I was already going to have to borrow money, and that was going to deplete me down to nothing. So, with the four-family continually being delayed and my other deals going on, I decided to back out of the six-family deal.

On the four-family, it turned out there were title issues, which complicated things in more ways than one, because my brother was going to move into this thing. He was planning to move into the first floor when it closed and he was basically going to live rent-free and take care of the building for me while I collected a little bit of money on the side. Again, this was going to be a great paycheck for me in the long run and I knew it.

That was the plan. But here's what really happened.

There were some holes in the exterior of the four-family, and before I could close on it, FHA required me to repair all of the holes in the vinyl siding that was allowing birds to get into the attic. I explained to the seller that I couldn't get an FHA loan unless the hole was fixed, and I asked him to take care of it for me. He refused. He told me it was an amazing deal and I should go with a conventional payment option, but I couldn't finance it another way, nor could my brother, so I ended up having to spend $3,000 to get the whole exterior fixed up and wrapped up so that it would pass FHA. At this point, since I'd thrown three grand at it without even closing yet, I had quite a bit more skin in the game than on any of my other deals.

Finally, we're getting close to the closing table and I'm slapped with a title issue. The house wasn't foreclosed properly. My attorney and his attorney were working together to fix this as the signing got pushed from one month to the next to the next, delay after delay. About three or four months into trying to finalize this deal, the seller came to me and said, "Hey, the market has gone up in value. I have this thing under agreement with you for $150K, but I could easily put it on the market for

$180K now, especially since you've already put your money into fixing it for FHA."

He was right and I knew it. It wasn't a smart idea for me to put the money in without having the deal closed, and it wasn't the first time I'd done this. I'd gotten lucky the first time, and there was no certainty I'd be that lucky again. It looked like I was going to lose this deal and the three grand I'd dropped on it after putting in all this effort and after giving up my six-family deal to make this one work.

For anybody who's ever tried to buy a house and have it not work out the right way, like a short sale, you know how stressful it is to not be able to close when you want to close. You want to know for sure when you're going to get it and get your money and get your renovations going. So, needless to say, I was already stressed out even before the seller dropped this bomb on me.

Here I am in this situation, an agent representing myself and the seller bypassing his agent to work directly with me, which is an uncomfortable and inappropriate situation, but it's how he wanted to handle it. I remember the emotional phone call, I was clear with him and said, "Look, it's in your best interest to work with me." He told me he was tired of waiting to close and I pulled at his pride. "Just be honorable. You said you were going to sell me the house. I put in all this effort, and I've waited all this time. I genuinely want to close and take care of this property and fix all the tenant issues. Please, be honorable and go through with our deal."

It was strenuous and he didn't want to do any of the work – he didn't want to fix the smoke detectors or do anything with the property – so I ended up spending another $600 getting them fixed on top of the $600 I dropped for the appraisal and the other $3,000 I'd dropped repairing the hole, and the extra money I dropped for the home inspection, which should have been $600, but my home inspector is a really good friend of mine who gives a great deal to anybody who works with me, and he cut me a deal after I told him everything I'd gone through with this property.

There was a lot of stress leading up to the closing, but the day we closed was one of the most relieving moments of my life. Closing on this one had brought me up to 13 units, past my goal of having 12 units for that year. I'd broken past that, hitting 13 units, and I could finally start renovating it for my brother.

We worked on all the carpets, patched all the holes, repaired the kitchen and some things in the bathroom. We made it through a lot of the renovation, when tragedy struck our family.

My grandfather had fallen and hit his head. He was in the hospital with internal bleeding in his brain, and my grandmother was diagnosed with pancreatic cancer at the same time. My brother decided that he didn't was to leave his apartment right above our grandparents in my grandfather's four-family. He thought he'd be better off staying there in case they ever needed him for something. It didn't make sense for him to move out of his apartment and into one of mine on the other side of the city. I completely agreed with that, but that decision put me in a stressful situation again.

I've got winter coming. My brother doesn't want to take that unit. I have another tenant who is a pain to work with and isn't paying. I'm having a hard time with this building in seven ways, like déjà vu. This happens in real estate. You'll have a family member, friend or even a new tenant who's going to move in, then suddenly they don't want to move in, and you are back to the drawing board. I put it back up on Craigslist and was getting no hits.

Finally, I get somebody who wants to move in, we sign the lease, get everything read, and the day she's in there cleaning, she called me up and said, "I'm so sorry, but my daughters don't like this apartment. We don't like the way this is set up and I want my money back."

At this point, I'd taken a month to renovate it, another month to market it, and now I was about to lose another month because it's going to take even longer to get another tenant in there. We came up with a compromise – since she'd been saying for 14 days that she was going to move into the unit, she would get a partial refund, to which she understood and readily agreed.

Having half a month's rent was helpful, but I was still in a position where I was missing a tenant. Now I was spending all my time shopping for tenants while I worked, and I clearly wasn't very good at finding tenants. During this time I wasn't able to pay much attention to my real estate business, where I was actually making more money as a real estate agent.

I'd been able to close 13 deals between June, July, and August, but my business was starting to slow down because of all the stress of this property. I was taking time off of selling to instead focus on getting my portfolio together – getting all of my units rented, getting the single-family rented, getting the storefront fixed, and getting this four-family that I'd just closed on fixed up and rented. All of that was taking away from my real estate business, so my girlfriend at the time stepped in around October and said, "I'm going to help you out and find a good tenant, that way you can get back to making money."

She was a blessing. I'd gone two months without making money because I'd been too focused on doing all the work for the renovation, stuff I didn't really belong doing and now I teach our students to not fall into that trap. We make more money doing sales, and if we make more money doing our own business, then we should pay somebody else to do the things we don't make money doing.

Now, I have leasing agents who handle all my leasing for me. I have property managers who handle all the property management tasks. I have maintenance guys who go out and maintain everything. I could have done it back in October of 2016, too, but I didn't know I could. So there I was, losing all this money or not making money because I was trying to stop the bleeding, when in reality I should have been making money and having a good team in place to take care of the things I don't enjoy.

Don't make the mistakes I made. As a landlord, learn this from your real estate mentor: make sure that you put property management in place so they can handle everything for you. They'll handle the leasing, they'll handle the maintenance, and most importantly they'll handle the phone calls.

I didn't have somebody to teach me that, so I had to learn from my own mistakes. But you have the opportunity to learn from mine, so make sure you don't forget these things.

Finally, I was able to get a great tenant in there and the unit finally started paying $1,000 per month, which meant I was making about $400 from the building each month now. By putting this tenant in, everything was back up and my entire portfolio was rented just in time for winter. It was right around November or December when we finally got them in there, and I started getting back into the flow of the money game, where properties were cash flowing, which is always where you want to be.

Taking on a new property is always tough because you end up losing money for the first couple of months, pretty much like starting a new business, but once everything is loaded up and fixed, the bleeding stops and cash flow becomes inevitable.

Having full units in the winter is vital, especially here in New England, where winters can cause a lot of problems if pipes freeze or you're paying heat to make sure they don't and it's an additional cost. So, it was a tough year, but it was a great year. Growth isn't always easy. I brought in a lot of new agents, bought a few properties, learned a few new tricks, and by the end of the year I realized that I never want to work that hard or stress that much ever again.

I've since spent my time building better systems, hiring a better property manager, training my teams to run my business without me and I took on a business partner to help grow our portfolio, training company and real estate brokerage, because I will never run myself ragged like I did in 2016. It was a year that made me money and made me strong. It changed my entire perception on how to make money and how much work I actually need to do.

Ask yourself this question often:

-Does this need to be done by ME or is there someone else who can do it better and faster while I do what pays me the most?

OUTROS

That brings us to 2017, which after accumulating 13 apartments, a team of 25 real estate agents and a gross income of $250k which in 2016 I'll owe nearly $60k in taxes on. The more important factor is the equity in my buildings which in 2017 added up to around $250,000. If you remember at the beginning of this book, after the divorce I was left with a debt of -$25,000 and in 2 short years was able to increase not only income, but net-worth as well which is a true measure of wealth.

My wish is that you recognize that no matter where you are in life that you will only be a stronger person this year, because you will learn from your past experiences, and will gain new perspective on the way this game of life is truly played and measured.

This is only the first part of my story – it's something I've been meaning to put together in one place for you for a long time. I have a tendency to tell the same story over and over, and it's nice to finally get it out and put it somewhere that you can read and get an idea of what is possible, where I came from, and how I became the man that I am today.

No, you don't need to come from money. You don't need to come from a family of successful real estate investors or real estate agents. You can build this, because you can build yourself. You can have more, because you can become more than you have been. You can learn how real estate works and make it a part of your life.

This story was put together to motivate you, to remind you that it is possible for you to be successful. You don't have to be the sharpest tool in the shed. I certainly wasn't. I had terrible grades. You don't have to be social or outspoken to be great at sales. I was homeschooled, so I wasn't well socialized, but sales is a trainable skill. What I've become, what I've built, was out of a desire to be a better person, to add value to people's lives, and to be a bigger part of my community.

Now I want to teach people what is possible for them, but first I had to prove to myself that it was possible, and now that I've done that, I'm thankful that I can inspire others through this story to do the same, and hopefully to do it even better.

I created the training company Agent Alchemist because I know what it's like to start in this business and not know the right things to do to be successful. In our live training events we bring you through a series of experiential learning exercises to help guide you through the process of increasing your income and your money blueprint. You will learn the principles behind an abundance mindset and how you can increase your sales skills through proven methods which we are constantly testing with our teams who are still actively in the field.

As important as learning sales is going to be for you to reach your financial freedom I focused primarily in this book on the emotional struggles and the real estate investments because in the long run those are the two most important pieces to the puzzle. You can learn more about our online training for real estate investors at GualterAmarelo.com as well as look for upcoming events in your area. At our live events we focus on the practical tools you need as well as the emotional tools you will use to be able to pull the trigger on the right deals and to keep you motivated through your journey.

Building wealth and mentoring other to do the same is what I've always wanted to do and I am thankful to have you on this journey with me. So, even though you have big challenges in your life. I want you to know that there's a way to learn whatever it takes to overcome that hurdle, and if you never stop growing, you can become a bigger person, so big to the point that the challenge is never a problem ever again.

It's not the problem or the size of the challenge – it's always the size of you. If you can be bigger than that challenge, then the challenge is now small in comparison.

It has been a great honor to be able to spend this time with you. If yourself in the beautiful city of Fall River make sure you check out one of the Agent Alchemist events. This is a city on the rise. I intent to continue investing and building businesses here and I encourage you to join me in building your empire here with me.

So, from my story to yours, remember, never stop improving, never stop learning, never stop moving forward, and when you have a choice, always work with the best.

MOST IMPORTANT TAKEAWAYS

- Seek out mentors now and often
- Be aware of the strain your goals will put on the people closest to you.
- Your single-family home is not an investment.
- Don't quit your job until you have created enough passive income to support you.
- When you think you are listening, stop and listen.
- Have a positive mindset and seek the things you want.
- Price is Relative, Never buy on a main street, Never buy a house without a basement
- Does this need to be done by ME or is there someone else who can do it better and faster while I do what pays me the most?
- Read something every day, and make them books that will help you grow in the direction you want to grow.
- If you don't change yourself, you won't change your income.

MOST IMPORTANT TAKEAWAYS

- Always get back up. Falling down is never an excuse to stop moving forward.

- With every great failure, there's an even greater comeback waiting to be made.

- Never stop Improving.

- Never stop Learning.

- Never stop Moving Forward.

- When you have a choice, always work with the best.

Resources:

    GualterAmarelo.com   AgentAlchemist.com

Made in United States
North Haven, CT
19 January 2022